My Brother's Keeper

Union and Confederate Soldiers' Acts of Mercy during the Civil War

Daniel N. Rolph

To Ben Erlacher — With best wishes, Daniel N. Rolph 8/war/2002

STACKPOLE
BOOKS

Published by
STACKPOLE BOOKS
5067 Ritter Road
Mechanicsburg, PA 17055
www.stackpolebooks.com

Printed in the United States of America

10 9 8 7 6 5 4 3 2 1

FIRST EDITION

Library of Congress Cataloging-in-Publication Data

Rolph, Daniel N., 1953–
    My brother's keeper : Union and Confederate soldiers' acts of mercy during the Civil War / Daniel N. Rolph.— 1st ed.
        p. cm.
    Includes bibliographical references and index.
    ISBN 0-8117-0997-3
    1. United States—History—Civil War, 1861–1865—Social aspects—Anecdotes. 2. Soldiers—United States—Social conditions—19th century—Anecdotes. 3. Soldiers—Confederate States of America—Social conditions—Anecdotes. 4. Civil-military relations—United States—History—19th century—Anecdotes. 5. Mercy—Anecdotes. 6. Kindness—Anecdotes. I. Title.

E468.9 .R65 2002
973.7'1—dc21
                                                                    2001049742

DEDICATION

To my wife Jeanette: a "Southern California Belle," who encouraged me, more than anyone, to write this book and who, beyond doubt, is the most kind and compassionate person I have ever known.

For I was an hungered, and ye gave me meat:
I was thirsty, and ye gave me drink:
I was a stranger, and ye took me in:
naked, and ye clothed me:
I was sick, and ye visited me:
I was in prison, and ye came unto me.

—Matt. 25:35–36

A good way to judge people
is by observing how they
treat those who can do them
absolutely no good.

—Anonymous

CONTENTS

THE DYING REBEL

On a Summer's morn, in a Southern clime,
While the sun shone bright o'er Hatteras bay,
Through a gate of the captured fort we marched,
And came where the dying soldiers lay.
And there, in the sight of our stars and stripes,
Hung the rebel flag from a broken mast.
Where a gallant youth, near a blood-stained tent,
On a bed of straw and breathing his last.
We paused at his side as the ranks closed in,
While the weary guard trod silent and slow,
Till no sound was heard but the feeble moan,
That arose from the lips of the wounded foe.
And as the last throbs of his faint pulse beat,
A death-like quiver ran over his breast;
And a lone word burst from his happy soul,
When the prayer went up for his future rest.
Twas a solemn scene, as we gathered there,
And gazed while the tears from many eyes fell;
For low at our feet wept the mangled brave,
Whose life was wrecked by a bursting shell.
Yet we boasted not of our glory and power,
As backward he fell on his gory bed;
For a whisper passed like an angel's voice,
And his spirit freed, from the battles fled.

—Marshall S. Pike

PREFACE

THOUGH *MY BROTHER'S KEEPER: UNION AND CONFEDERATE SOLDIERS' Acts of Mercy during the Civil War*, utilizes primary source materials such as diaries, letters, military reports, newspapers, etc., as well as secondary resources, it is not meant to be a scholarly treatise. Its main purpose is simply to reveal, to scholar and lay person alike, a unique and little-known genre of Civil War history.

Regarding the sources employed, the author has preferred to use verbatim quotations from original authors as much as possible, rather than to paraphrase. While, at times, this approach has resulted in lengthy narratives, such renditions are intended to capture the essence and spirit of those who experienced the war firsthand.

With respect to source material, the author has taken the liberty, in some but not all cases, to alter the text—as it applies to paragraph structure, capitalization, punctuation, spelling, etc.—but in no way to "improve" or add text where none existed. Also, in many cases, the original sources misspelled surnames, gave incorrect regimental designations and dates for engagements, or simply told little or nothing about the outfit and rank of those quoted. The author has consulted public documents and secondary sources, too numerous to cite within the endnote section or bibliography, to fill in these gaps.

If readers have questions concerning source material for the accounts contained within this volume and would like to correspond with the author, they should feel free to do so. Contact can be made through the publisher. The author also looks forward to hearing from individuals who can share similar accounts uncovered throughout their own research.

ACKNOWLEDGMENTS

No book or monograph can be written or published without the help, expertise, and encouragement of many people. Though it is impossible to thank every individual involved in the completion of *My Brother's Keeper*, I would be inconsiderate and ungrateful not to at least mention the following for their support.

I am particularly thankful to the publisher, Stackpole Books, and their editorial staff (both named and unnamed), who have patiently worked with me on this project. First of all I thank William C. Davis and the Editorial Board for responding positively to this work, but particularly to editor Leigh Ann Berry, with whom I have had the most contact, for her encouragement, critical and professional advice, and willingness to work with me, despite my inadequate knowledge of current technologies in the world of publishing. I also wish to extend thanks to Michelle M. Simmons, Ryan Masteller, and others of the editorial staff, whom I do not know, but with whom I have corresponded or who worked on the actual editing of the manuscript.

I am especially grateful to Marion Egge, a professional editor and author as well, with whom I have collaborated before on writing projects, and who made this work possible in its initial stages. She has been a friend, coworker, and advisor for many years, to whom I am deeply indebted.

I wish to thank the Historical Society of Pennsylvania, for the opportunity to work at such a remarkable institution, and to enjoy both personally and professionally its valuable collections relating to the Civil War and other genres. I am especially grateful to the former Graphic Archivist and head of the Rights and Reproductions Department at HSP, Bruce Scherer, and photographer Lou Meehan, for their prompt response to my requests and permission to reproduce various photographs and selections from manuscript collections available at the Historical Society in Philadelphia.

Ronald A. Lee of the Tennessee State Library and Archives; author Mark Reynolds; Stacy Hartman of Longstreet Press; Allen Stokes of the South Caroliniana Library in Columbia; Don Phanz and Karlton D. Smith of the National Park Service; Richmond Camera of Fredericksburg, Virginia; Broadfoot Publishing of Wilmington, North Carolina, to name a few, have made some of the selections and photographs contained within this volume a possibility. I also wish to express appreciation to the Civil War Library and Museum of Philadelphia, whose collections, volunteers, and employees, such as Steve Zerby and former curator Steve Wright, who were always ready and willing to aid me in my researching pursuits.

Last, but certainly not least, I thank my wife, Jeanette, and children, Joshua, Sarah, Benjamin, Mary, and John, as well as my son and daughter-in-law, Shawn and Kristina, along with my parents, Nelson and Ruth Rolph, and sister Brenda DeYoung, as well as a numerous host of other relatives and friends, who gave me the moral support, encouragement, and desire to persevere through this enterprise. Those not named are in no way unappreciated.

Also, I thank those brave men and women, both Union and Confederate, who amidst horrendous conditions, still personified what it truly means to be "My Brother's Keeper," whose exemplary lives made this book a possibility.

INTRODUCTION

THROUGHOUT HISTORY, SOLDIERS ON OPPOSING SIDES HAVE DONE surprising things, many of them in direct opposition to the normal activities associated with warfare. During the Third Crusade, Richard I of England, better known as "Richard the Lion-Hearted," arrived at the scene of the battle of Jaffa (August 5, 1192) on foot. An Islamic warrior, Seifeddin, son of Richard's arch enemy, Saladin, graciously sent "two war-horses to King Richard," who "gratefully accepted them and used them."[1] Saladin and other Islamic leaders are said to have actually paid the ransom for their own Christian prisoner, the knight Sir Hugo of Tabarie, because he had honorably returned to be executed when he failed to acquire the funds needed to obtain his freedom.[2]

On a more personal level, I can vividly recall an experience from my own youth when, at about age fourteen, I witnessed a personal reunion of two former enemies. My father, Nelson F. Rolph, who had served in the 36th Infantry Division during World War II, was asked to visit a gentleman in a community some forty miles from our home in Northeastern Kentucky. Though I can no longer recall his name, he had served in a German infantry regiment during the war, and at one time had fought against my father's outfit in battle. To hear the two men converse about that war and their experiences, it was as if they had been comrades in arms rather than on opposing sides.

Also during World War II, POW Gene DuVall recalled his "most memorable Christmas," while incarcerated in winter 1944 at Stalag VII-A in Moosburg, Germany, where German guards and prisoners of war celebrated

1

the holiday together.[3] Similarly, John H. Moffitt, an American POW at Stalag XVII-B outside Krems, Austria, recalls how one inmate was shot while trying to escape. A funeral procession composed of the German guards as well as the soldier's friends marched to the cemetery, where the body was placed "in a wooden casket with an American flag draped over it. After the funeral, the German soldiers fired a volley over the grave."[4]

Such humanitarianism and hospitality are generally rare or nonexistent in military conflicts. The Civil War, however, is an exception to the rule. Though vengeance, atrocities, inhumanity, and cruelties did indeed transpire during the war; simultaneously, even in the midst of battle, noble virtues and sentiments were manifested many times. Such actions ignored political ideologies, crossed sectional or regional boundaries, and transcended all gender, class, and racial barriers.

The work of doctors and nurses in both the Union and Confederate armies, along with humanitarian organizations such as the Christian Sanitary Commission and Volunteer Refreshment Saloons, is well known; but the many individual "Good Samaritan" acts of kindness and generosity of common soldiers and citizens toward their enemies are largely unfamiliar to both the scholar and the general public. Both "Rebels" and "Yankees" were by and large raised from the cradle to the grave on the same fundamental values and principles contained within the Judeo-Christian Bible. At a time when honor and chivalry were virtues not only to be idealized but also emulated, it is little wonder that such cases of human charity and compassion did indeed occur.

Writing from the headquarters of the Army of the Potomac stationed at Warrington, Virginia, on October 21, 1863, Maj. James Cornell Biddle of the 27th Pennsylvania Infantry related to his wife, Gertrude Meredith Biddle of Philadelphia, the following incident concerning his opponent, Confederate general Robert E. Lee:

> Lee followed on a parallel line with us as far as Broad Run and as soon as we got in his front, and advanced against him he retreated, he remained for one night at this place.
>
> An old lady living here went to see him. She put out her hand, and told him it had never touched a Yankee, and commenced abusing our troops. Lee they say rebuked her, and told her he was sorry to hear her speak in that way, that there were a great many gentlemen in our

army, and some of those whom she mentioned were men whom he had a very great esteem for, and were formerly his most cherished friends.

The officers whom he took prisoners were allowed to remain in a house at this place and upon promising not to attempt to escape, to hire a wagon to take them to Culpepper without any guard.[5]

Later, writing from Burksville Junction, Major Biddle would remark how it "is a very different feeling in the Army, from that which exists amongst civilians, who have never heard a bullet whistle."[6] This thought was aptly echoed by Seth Flint, who had served in the 5th U.S. Cavalry, and was present at the surrender of Lee and the Army of Northern Virginia at Appomattox Courthouse on April 9, 1865. Speaking of the event, he emphatically declared his belief that if Abraham Lincoln had been spared "there would have been no Reconstruction," for he would have "like Grant . . . grasped the hands of those soldiers in Confederate gray and welcomed them back home. . . . Soldiers don't carry hatred; they leave that to the stay-at-homes. We learned that in the next twenty years."[7] As one officer had remarked as late as July 1864, "Yes, yes, indeed, . . . if the settlement of this thing were left to our armies there would be peace and good fellowship established in two hours."[8]

Such absence of animosity toward one's enemy would be demonstrated, even amid the roar of cannon and musketry, throughout many of the battles, engagements, and skirmishes of the American Civil War. The appalling scenes of the maimed, wounded, and dying, as well as their cries of distress and pain, caused many a veteran soldier on both sides to forget his own safety or welfare to administer aid or comfort to an enemy in need. His humanity, not the color of his uniform or political persuasion, became at times the overriding issue. As one Confederate nurse remarked, "Seeing an enemy wounded and helpless, is a different thing from seeing him in health and in power."[9]

This philanthropic philosophy was aptly summarized in an account recorded after the war by a Mr. William Wilkerson of Fayette County, Kentucky, of an experience he witnessed. After the battle of Richmond, Kentucky, fought on August 30, 1862, Wilkerson was riding over the battlefield in an attempt to locate and identify the body of a friend—so he could "take it to his father's home." He states:

I heard groans, which I was sure came from a cornfield near at hand. Looking down the corn rows I soon discovered two wounded soldiers lying about forty yards apart. One was a Federal and the other was a Confederate. A cannon ball had broken and terribly mangled both of the Confederate's legs, while the Federal was shot through the body and thigh.

"I am dying for water," I heard the Federal say, just as I discovered them. His words sounded as if they came from a parched mouth.

"I have some water in my canteen. You are welcome to a drink if you'll come here," said the Confederate, who had feebly raised his head from the ground to look at his late enemy when he heard his pitiful cry for water.

"I couldn't move to save my life," groaned the Federal, as he dropped his head to the ground, while his whole body quivered with agony.

Then I beheld an act of heroism which held me spellbound until it was too late for me to give the assistance I should have rendered. The Confederate lifted his head again, and took another look at his wounded foe, and I saw an expression of tender pity come over his pain-distorted face as he said:

"Hold out a little longer, Yank, and I'll try to come to you." Then the brave fellow, by digging his fingers in the ground and catching hold of the cornstalks, painfully dragged himself to the Federal's side, the blood from his mangled legs making a red trail the entire distance.

The tears ran down my cheeks like rain, and out of sympathy for him, I groaned every time he moved, but I was so lost to everything except the fellow's heroism that I did not once think of helping him.

When the painful journey was finished he offered his canteen to the Federal, who took it and drank eagerly, the water seeming to sizzle as it passed down his parched throat.

Then, with a deep sign of relief, he reached out to the Confederate, and it was plain to see as they clasped hands and looked into each other's eyes that whatever of hate may have rankled once in the hearts of these men had now given place to mutual sympathy and love. Even while I watched them I saw the Confederate's body quiver as if in a spasm of pain, and when his head dropped to the ground I knew that a hero had crossed the dark river.

The Federal kissed the dead hero's hand repeatedly, and cried like a child until I had removed him to the hospital, where he, too, died the next day.[10]

The above account, in many ways, captures the essence of this book. It demonstrates that the Civil War is not just about military campaigns, tactics, strategies, and hostile political creeds. The Civil War portrays individuals who, with differing opinions under horrendous conditions, could nevertheless show compassion and respect for one another as human beings, as in the timeless Biblical tale of the "Good Samaritan," a lesson too often ignored in today's litigious, politically correct environment.

The following narratives will present to the reader an important though rarely discussed aspect of Civil War history. Yet it is the desire of the author, also, to emphasize the practical relevance and application these stories should have—for both family and national conflicts occurring within our modern era. For the reality of Alexander Pope's observation has lost none of its luster over the years: "To err is human, to forgive divine."

CHAPTER 1

Fraternizing with the Enemy

SCATTERED THROUGHOUT DIARIES, LETTERS, AND CONTEMPORARY publications of the Civil War are numerous accounts of Union and Confederate soldiers conversing, trading, and even visiting one another's camps during lulls in battle or on picket duty. Oral traditions preserved among the descendants of Civil War soldiers also substantiate the reality of such incidents.

A relative of the author, Jackson Brewer, a prisoner of war at both Libby Prison in Virginia and at Andersonville, Georgia, who served in Co. K, 23rd Kentucky Infantry (Union), remarked that "during times of truce they [the Yankees] would bum or trade off tobacco with the rebels."[1] A granddaughter of Franklin Boyts, Co. C, 142nd Regiment of Pennsylvania Volunteers, recalled,

> I well remember him . . . and as a young child sitting on his knee, I would ask him to tell me something of the War. . . .
>
> The only thing he ever told me was of a simple incident, when he and a young Confederate soldier sat together by a muddy roadside in the rain—during some lull in hostilities. [T]hey shared their scant rations—salt pork and soda crackers. I felt that they shared much more in that brief interlude.[2]

The good humor existing during hostilities is demonstrated by Lt. Col. Oliver Hopkinson, of the 51st Pennsylvania Militia Regiment and 1st Delaware Infantry. Writing home to his wife Lizzy from a "camp before Fredericksburg," in Virginia on November 24, 1862, the Federal officer stated, "Our pickets and the Rebel pickets . . . converse freely. Yesterday the N. Carolina pickets on the other side proposed to ours [New Hampshire Regiment] that if we "would hang up Abe Lincoln on our side of the stream, they would fetch Jeff Davis and hang him up on theirs."[3]

At the battle of Murfreesboro (Stone's River) on December 31, 1862, one of Union general William S. Rosecrans's men related "One of the most remarkable features of this war is the absence of vindictiveness among the soldiery of the two sections. When parties have met with flags of truce, the privates will freely converse, drink from each other's canteens, and even have a friendly game of cards in a fence corner. Especially upon picket duty has this friendliness broken in upon discipline—so much so that in many instances orders have been issued strictly forbidding such intercourse." [4]

Concerning Murfreesboro, a member of the 8th Kentucky (Union) related an incident of December 28 at Stewart's Creek, some ten miles from the city. After firing a few random shots at one another, individuals on picket duty finally "quit shooting," and concluded they would "talk it out." A conversation then occurred between a Federal and a Confederate:

> Federal (at the top of his voice)—Hello, boys: what regiment?
> Confederate—8th Confederate. What's your regiment?
> F.—8th and 21st Kentucky.
> C.—All right.
> F.—Boys, have you got any whiskey?
> C.—Plenty of her.
> F.—How'll you trade for coffee?
> C.—Would like to accommodate you, but never drink it while the worm goes.
> F.—Let's meet at the creek and have a social chat.
> C.—Will you shoot?
> F.—Upon the honor of a gentleman, not a man shall. Will you shoot?
> C.—I give you as good assurance.
> F.—Enough said. Come on.

C.—Leave your arms.

F.—I have left them. Do you leave yours?

C.—I do. . . .

Thus the conversation went on for some time, until a Confederate captain (Miller, of General Wheeler's cavalry) came down, requesting an exchange of newspapers. . . . Some compliments were passed, when the captain suggested that, as it was getting late, we have better quit the conference; whereupon both parties, about twenty each, began to leave, with "Good bye, [B]oyd; if ever I meet you in battle, I'll spare you." So we met and parted, not realizing that we were enemies. [5]

Sgt. Joseph N. Pattison of a Delaware regiment related that he and "a Southern soldier on picket duty swapped newspapers and chewin' tobacco,"[6] while James and Abraham Sturgis of the 85th Pennsylvania Infantry, stationed in Tennessee during the summer of 1863, fraternized with Rebel troops of Confederate general Jubal Early "at Meadow Bluffs," on the east side of "Big Sorrell Mountain." Abraham recalled:

The fraternal commingling of the blue and gray was both interesting and amusing, and the exchange of jacknives, spurs, buttons, rations, etc., freely and generously concluded. It was wonderful to note the mollifying influence of that little white flag. Men who under the ordinary circumstances of war would have been trying to visit death and destruction on each other by all the appliances known to modern carnage, now seemed as friendly as tho no war storm had ever disturbed the contending sections or aroused the passions that caused the hand of man to be lifted against his brother. . . .[7]

Contemporary newspaper accounts in 1863 also reveal the lack of animosity, at times, between the opposing armies. One Northern editorial, appearing not long after the battle of Vicksburg, remarked:

After the taking of Vicksburg there was a general fraternization of the soldiers of the two armies, and they mingled with each other unrestrainedly, discussed the war, expressed their regret that it was not over, and manifested toward each other the cordiality and good feeling of old companions in arms, instead of exhibiting the hatred and reserve of enemies.

The same thing was observed at Port Hudson. The men who the day before were shooting the balls at each other, immediately after the surrender shared the rations, entered into friendly chat, and discussed the campaign with more philosophical coolness than two political opponents can exhibit over any partisan subject. There were plenty of jokes but no taunts. . . . *Each side had learned to respect the other, as brave men will always respect brave men.* Each was resolute in maintaining his own views to be right, but there was no rancor, no malevolent feeling, nothing which would indicate that the animosities between them were of such an irreconcilable character that they could not live in the same political Union together.

The fact is, the rebellion did not arise from any regional hatred between the people of the two sections. With them the differences were political and not personal.[8]

Regarding Port Hudson, an article entitled "Fraternization" recalled:

All accounts agree that the Federal and Rebel forces at Port Hudson, immediately upon our occupation of the place, fraternized in the kindest possible manner, apparently forgetting entirely that they had ever been arrayed in hostile columns. It was precisely thus, also at Vicksburg, at Gettysburg, and on every other field where the men have been brought together in the hush or at the close of conflict.

Those persons who are fond of insisting that the people of the South and those of the North can never be reconciled or live together in peace when the war is done and the spirit of rebellion is destroyed, will hardly find in facts like these we have cited a confirmation of their argument.[9]

Capt. John P. Green, a staff officer in the Federal army, 2nd Brigade, 1st Division, XII Army Corps, wrote from Bridgeport, Alabama, in 1864, recalling an incident of the "Battle above the Clouds," or battle of Lookout Mountain—Missionary Ridge in Tennessee, fought November 23–25, 1863:

> The thing that impresses you most strongly is that the men in the field have no bitter feeling toward each other, and would be glad to stop fighting and shake hands at any moment. When we had scaled Lookout Mountain and were resting on the summit, a couple of Indiana Regiments were fighting the Rebs about two hundred yards below us.
>
> Each side was sheltered by rocks and the men were popping away whenever a head showed itself, but in the intervals you would hear them shout, "Halloo Yank!" "Halloo Reb!" "Got any coffee?" Bang! goes a musket, followed by a sharp volley. "Got any tobacco?" "Yes!" or "No!" as the case might be; and you would have laughed to hear them in the best humor in the world, calling out to stop shooting and come out and make the exchange. The pickets do this constantly, but I never saw it done in a fight before.[10]

Writing from Cold Harbor, Virginia, in June 1864, Rebel sergeant William J. Mosely, Co. D, 10th Georgia Infantry (C.S.A.), mentioned a "cessation of hostilities," so that the dead could be buried after the battle of the twenty-seventh. He stated:

> We all felt like I imagine a bird feels when let out of a cage, ours and the enemy's lines were about 150 yards apart, and we would meet the Yankees on the half way ground, and exchange papers and talk with them, like we had always been friends, we draw tobacco now and we can get anything we want from them with it, one of our men got a fine knife from them [for] a plug and a half.[11]

their points. I can assure you that this Reb did not out-talk me. We parted good friends and bid each other good-bye. He said that he had been in Philadelphia on several occasions and it was a very nice city and nice people.[13]

Still stationed at Petersburg in 1864, Corporal Smith once again wrote home on August 7 and described events occurring while on picket duty:

I was on picket yesterday and had a chat with three Rebs at a big walnut tree 30 yards in front of picket line. To get there, we crawl down a ravine so our officers do not see us. I went with two other soldiers who were pickets. Here we met several Rebs who came 50 yards by the same ravine to meet us. It was "Hello, Yank" and "Hello, Johnny, what you got to trade?" Our men want tobacco and they want sugar and coffee, thread, etc.

Another rebel said to me, "Have you got any green-backs over your side?" "Plenty," I replied. "Wish you would make a charge on us so we can get some money. I got $400 from your dead in the Wilderness Battle."

It is terrible to think how they plunder and rob the dead of money and clothing. . . . So many scenes and incidents took place under this few hour's truce, and when the time was up, each side ran for their lines and firing was resumed, each side doing their best to shoot each other.[14]

Performing picket duty on August 12, Smith mentions that he "traded with a Rebel soldier some coffee for tobacco and papers. . . . This rebel belonged to the 2nd Florida; his name is Lumpkins."[15] Though unknown to Corporal Smith, this particular Confederate, who served in Co. G or the "St. Johns Grays," of the 2nd Florida Infantry, was later wounded at Petersburg in September, lost part of his left thigh from amputation at a local general hospital, and was buried in October 1864 at the Blandford Cemetery.[16]

Corporal Smith continued his account of picket duty for August 12:

We crawl down a ravine that is covered with brush and our officers and their officers do not see them, and here we have a talk and do a little trading. They need and are anxious to get needles, thread, cotton, haversacks, picture papers, and are willing to pay Yankee money for the same, which they have secured from our dead soldiers in various battles. Yesterday, there were seven Rebels there and the last time there were four down and four of our men. We stayed there for one hour chatting with them. . . .

One of them said, "Hello, you're a fine looking chap," and I said, "Hello, Johnnie." He laughed at that name and asked me what state I was from. I told him I was a Philadelphia boy. He said he was born in Philadelphia, across from the Arch Street Theatre. He is now a courier on Gen. Mahone's Staff. He . . . spoke to me of many places in Philadelphia. . . .

I went down this ravine six times yesterday and traded papers and other things for tobacco and pocket knives and handkerchiefs, and as we parted we shook hands with the usual salutes of, "Take care of yourself. Good-bye."[17]

Pvt. Whitsel Lewis of Co. A, 87th Indiana Infantry Regiment, writing in his diary during the siege of Atlanta on August 12, 1864 remarked:

We are on the front line at this time. Our men had bin trading with the rebs today. They have bin trading coffee for tobacco. Our men hollowed to the rebs and told them that they quit shooting for awhile and went half way between the line and done up their trading and came back to their rifle pits and went to shooting at each other again. I stood on the brest works and seen them come together and trade. it was a nice sight to see, their was a good many out to trade with the rebs today.[18]

The conversations between Federal and Confederate pickets were not limited exclusively to trading goods, but often centered upon politics as well. Lt. John W. Mitchell of Co. D, 12th New Jersey Infantry, spoke of a dialogue with a Rebel soldier at Petersburg in October 1864. He stated how he felt the Rebels' only hope lay "in the coming election." He further states:

Last evening I had a long talk with the Rebels on the picket line. They entertained great hopes of McClellan getting elected. They said he was going to have peace right away if he did. They think he will let them do as they please. After awhile they cheered for McClellan, and we cheered for Old Abe, and both parties went to firing again. Gen. Hancock sent an order out to be sent over to the Rebels. I tied it on the end of a ramrod and shot it over. It was an account of Sheridan's victory in the Valley, rather a queer way to send news over is it not.[19]

On occasion the fraternizing between troops of both armies became so amiable that their association with one another went way beyond that connected with picket duty. Pvt. W. B. McGinnis, of the "Iberville Grays" or Co. A, 3rd Louisiana Infantry, along with three other comrades, visited a Missouri Federal camp in Alabama near Mobile for a social drink and supper. A Federal lieutenant and guard, however, "interrupted . . . with orders to arrest the party for being within the Yankee lines." With the help of a New York captain and a Union major general, the Rebels were released and escorted back to their own lines, but not before they "emptied the canteens . . . by drinking each other's health. . . . They parted the best of friends, to endeavor to kill each other, if possible, the next day."[20]

On December 15, 1862, members of Daniel E. Sickles's famed "Excelsior Brigade," or the 70th through the 74th New York Infantry Regiments, fraternized with the enemy on the banks of the Rappahannock River. One Federal soldier remarked how the troops on picket duty began to converse with one another. The Rebels informed the Union soldiers that

[i]f our pickets would not fire they would not, and commenced to stand up and show themselves, and told our boys that there was a lot of wounded up there and for them to come and get them. In less time than it would take me to tell it, our boys and the Rebels were laughing and talking and shaking hands, trading coffee for tobacco and doing everything they could for one another.

A person to look at them would never suppose they had been enemies. . . . They were most all North Carolina troops, and were gentlemen and admitted more and done less blowing than any set of men that I have seen.[21]

Gen. John B. Gordon of the Confederate army recalled an incident about a lieutenant in a Delaware regiment, an officer of the picket line on the banks of the Rappahannock. He was invited by his Rebel counterpart to "come over after dark and go with him to a farm-house near the lines, where certain Confederates had invited country girls to a dance." A boat was provided, a suit of citizen's clothes lent to him, and he was told he would be sent "safely back to his own side before daylight the next morning." True to his word, the Confederate officer introduced his enemy to the girls at the dance as "a new recruit just arrived in camp," and the rest of the evening was spent dancing, after which he "was safely landed in his own lines before daylight."[22]

Maj. Henry Kyd Douglas, formerly of Stonewall Jackson's staff, related a "fraternizing expedition" taking place on the Virginia bank of the Potomac. This river was the dividing line between the two armies, as well as that separating Virginia from Maryland. The major's family resided on the Maryland side, and one day he was standing on the Virginia side and saw his father on the opposite shore in the garden. A Federal cavalry force also was in sight, who Douglas says, "saluted me by lifting their hats and I returned their salute." The friendly gestures continued, so that Douglas and a courier obtained a skiff and soon conversed with a half dozen Union soldiers on a ferryboat in the middle of the river. The Federals soon learned that Douglas was the "Captain Douglass [sic], of General Jackson's staff," and also one of the Rebel sons of "the old gentleman on the hill." Douglas related that the Union sergeant then demanded:

> With much earnestness, that I must get into their boat and go over to see my family. I began to protest that it would not do, when one of the others broke in: "Say, get in, captain; get in. If this Government can be *busted* up by a rebel soldier going to see his mother, why damn it, let it *bust*!

Douglas was soon reunited with his mother and beset with a host of Union soldiers full of questions about "Stonewall" Jackson. Upon leaving, the Confederate officer gave the sergeant and his crew his autograph "upon sundry slips of paper, and told them that if the fortune of war should make them prisoners, the little papers might be of service to them if sent to General Jackson's headquarters."

> As we took our leave and got into the skiff, the chivalric, manly sergeant said to me: "We belong to (I think) the 1st New York Cavalry. My parents live on the banks of the Hudson, and what I have done for you, I'd like some one to do for me if in the same fix. While I'm here I'll keep an eye on your home and people and do what I can for them" (and he did).
>
> And as the skiff moved over the water and took me from home again, I raised my hat to my "good friend, the enemy," and they stood along the shore, in response, with uncovered heads. . . . It is such touches as this that lighten up the inhumanities of war."[23]

Many other existing accounts detail the amiable relations of "Yankees" and "Rebels," on picket duty or while engaged in a multitude of diverse activities.[24] On one occasion Union and Confederate troops, "worked side by side . . . in perfect harmony, as if they never had been enemies," as they dug graves together after a battle[25] and played "a game of marbles" on a rainy day of June 1863 in the West Virginia mountains.[26]

Such acts of hospitality were not solely limited to selfish motives based on personal profit, gain, or pleasure, but at times were genuinely selfless acts of kindness and mercy, performed with the intention of alleviating distress or pain in a needy enemy brother.

CHAPTER 2

Freemasonry and Its "Brotherhood" in the Civil War

IT IS A WELL-KNOWN FACT THAT THE FRATERNAL ORGANIZATION OF THE Masonic Order, be it the York or the Scottish rite, has, both in times past and at the present day, carried out numerous acts of charity for many people. The members of the society have created a particular "brotherhood" by which they aid one another in times of trouble or distress. This fraternal care was acutely exemplified on many occasions during the Civil War, even toward the enemy, as witnessed by the following incidents.

Many of the soldiers in both the Union and Confederate armies were members of the Masonic Order. At times the Order was used as a political vehicle to rise in rank or prestige. Maj. James A. Congdon, 12th Pennsylvania Cavalry, speaks in his correspondence a number of times about the "Equality Lodge No. 136" of Martinsburg, Virginia, and of its influence within the regiment. He later remarked that an unpopular colonel, "through the political Masonic and other influence[,] will surely be reinstated."[1]

An intriguing account appears in the papers of Capt. Walter Symonds Newhall of Co. A, 3rd Pennsylvania Cavalry, 60th Regiment. In 1862, at a camp near Harrison's Landing, Virginia, he relates how, on June 30 while riding his horse, he was thrown against a stone wall and onto the ground. He was next confronted by "a tall man with long black hair, with the blue silk emblem of the Masons hanging over his shoulders." Newhall then queried:

"Stonewall" Jackson, says I? The same says he, at your service. The recollections of years flashed through my mind in a second. . . . I saw my escape and recalled the means of obtaining it.

"Who goes there?" says Jackson. "Friend with the countersign," I replied. "Advance friend and give the countersign commands the Chief." Here it was my memory saved me. I remembered the peculiar symbols of recognition among Masons as taught in "Midshipman Easy." I put my thumb to the end of my nose, gracefully twirled the remaining fingers in the air and was immediately answered, "Countersign is correct—advance friend."

Advancing in a confident way I remarked upon the singularity of his standing sentry instead of the soldiers— He replied he "was the soldiers" from which I inferred that he was the only man left in his division or else was the only reinforcement the Richmond Rebels had received—his name being as good as a small army—a very pardonable conceit considering the terror attaching to his name among us.

"We claim a great victory," I continued. I knew I could safely venture this remark for it wouldn't commit me to either side. Events have proved me correct in this. He observed "he didn't see it" which gave me his opinion in a few words. I mounted and hurried back, recovered my lost track, delivered my message and returned in safety to receive the salutes of the army as it opened upon the Enemy who had followed me to this Historic ground of Malvern Hills.[2]

Tradition has it that the "Rattle and Snap Mansion" at Ashwood, or Columbia, in Maury County, Tennessee, was saved during the Civil War because of the Masons. Yankees went into the home of slaveholder George Polk in order to burn it to the ground, but "there was a painting of the owner of the house, wearing a Masonic ring." Consequently, a member of the Federal army who was present revoked the order and refused to burn the dwelling since the Confederate owner was a Mason.[3]

The most dramatic accounts of Masonic brotherhood, however, concern the companionship exhibited by members toward one another on the battlefield, though they fought on opposite sides of the conflict. Frank Moore, in his famous postwar collection of Civil War songs and stories, recalls a touching incident that occurred the day after the "bloody battle" of Sharpsburg, or Antietam, Maryland, fought on September 17, 1862. The tale concerns a Lt. John Oden of Co. K, 10th Alabama Infantry, who lay wounded in a cornfield near the picket line of the 5th New Hampshire Infantry. Moore relates:

> Early in the morning one of the wounded rebels . . . called one of the New Hampshire men, and handed him a little slip of paper, on which he had, evidently with great difficulty, succeeded in making some mystic signs in a circle with a bit of stick wet in blood. The soldier was begged to give it to some Freemason as soon as possible, and he took it to Colonel E. E. Cross, of his regiment. The Colonel was a Master Mason, but could not read the mystic token, it belonging to a higher degree. He therefore sent for Captain J. B. Perry, of the fifth, who was a member of the thirty-second degree of Freemasonry, and showed him the letter. Captain Perry at once said there was a brother Mason in great peril, and must be rescued.
>
> He was found, placed on a blanket, and at great risk drawn out of range of the rebel rifles, and then carried to the Fifth New Hampshire hospital . . . badly wounded in the thigh and breast. A few hours and he would have perished. Lieutenant Edon [*sic*] informed his brethren of another wounded Mason, who, when brought out, proved to be a Lieutenant Colonel of a Georgia regiment. These two wounded rebel officers received the same attention as the wounded officers of the fifth, and a warm friendship was established between men who a few hours before were in mortal combat.[4]

Maj. Frederick L. Hitchcock of the 132nd Pennsylvania Volunteer Infantry, in the winter of 1862, became ill from "a severe attack of fever and ague." He was placed in an ambulance and eventually was housed at the farmhouse of a gentleman named D. L. F. Lake, a Confederate "guerrilla," a member of John S. Mosby's famous cavalry organization. Hitchcock describes how his host had definite secessionist sentiments, but his assistance to the Federal officer had been secured specifically "on the strength of Freemasonry." According to Hitchcock,

> His kindness to me on the score of our fraternal relations was generous to the full extent of his ability, and showed him to be a true man, notwithstanding his "secesh" proclivities. It was a great favor, for had I been compelled to remain out in that rough weather sick as I was, the consequences must have been most serious.
>
> On leaving I tried to pay him in gold coin for his hospitality, but he firmly declined my money, saying, "You know you could not have gotten into my house for money. Pay in like manner as you have received when opportunity affords." For this fraternal hospitality I shall always remember my "secesh" Masonic brother with gratitude, for I feel that it saved my life.[5]

During the battle of West Point, Virginia, on May 7, 1862, Cpl. James Cook of Co. F, 16th New York Infantry, had his leg "broken by a musket ball," and was left on the battlefield while the enemy temporarily occupied the location. A Rebel soldier stole his watch, purse, "and a Masonic ring," which caused Cook evidently to give the Masonic distress call. This cry for help brought to his side a Confederate Mason, who caused Cook's property to be restored to him, filled his canteen with water, made him as comfortable as possible, and on leaving, said, "we are enemies in honorable warfare, but on the plane where your disabilities have placed you the laws of humanity and charity prevail."[6]

After the second battle of Bull Run, or "Manassas," fought August 29–30, 1862, three Federal soldiers were left on the field by their comrades in the 10th New York Infantry Regiment. Capts. Robert A. Dimmick and Thomas D. Mosscrop, and Cpl. Edward A. Dubey, though badly wounded, were rescued by Capt. Hugh Barr of the 5th Regiment of Virginia Riflemen. Barr noticed a Masonic emblem worn by Mosscrop and thus gave the men special attention by summoning a surgeon who dressed the wounds of the enemy. The Union soldiers were taken to the Van Pell house nearby, a makeshift hospital, where their wounds healed and from where they were afterwards sent, not to a prison camp, but to Washington, D.C. Nineteen years later the three New Yorkers would record "for posterity, the kind act of the Virginia Mason, who, regarding a fallen foe as a friend in need, did all in his power to save their lives."[7]

A Civil War incident with a definite Masonic connection occurred on January 1, 1863, at Galveston, Texas, on the Gulf Coast. A number of accounts exist concerning the events, but it is sufficient to state that the Federal steam vessel, the *Harriet Lane,* commanded by Jonathan M. Wainwright of the U.S. Navy, was attacked and boarded by Confederate forces under the command of Maj. Gen. John B. Magruder. Wainwright was killed, along with Lt. Comdr. Edward Lea, while bravely defending their vessel.[8]

The ten-year-old son of Captain Wainwright was on board at the time of the engagement, and was "disabled by a ball shattering his four fingers" as he "stood at the cabin door . . . a revolver in his hand, and never ceased firing till he had expended every shot."[9] Maj. A. M. Lea, of the Confederate vessel *Bayou City,* upon boarding the Union steamer, discovered the body of his son, the aforementioned Federal officer Edward Lea, who "was mortally wounded, and only lived long enough to recognize his father, against whom he was fighting, before he died."[10]

On January 2, 1863, the minutes of Harmony Lodge No. 6 of Galveston record that a "Lodge of Emergency" was called "for the purpose of interring with the rite of Masonic burial," the body of Wainwright "who was killed in action while bravely fighting his vessel when it was captured 'by the blessing of God' by the forces of our Confederate government. . . . Officers of that vessel, now prisoners of war, had made themselves known as Master Masons, and vouched that the deceased was a regular Master Mason . . . in good standing. . . . [As such,] they besought at our hands a Masonic burial."[11]

Ironically, Wainwright was buried in the Episcopal Cemetery "with the rites of Masons," a ceremony attended by Maj. Gen. John B. Magruder of the Confederacy, as well as Master of the Lodge, P. C. Tucker, a major in the Rebel army who was serving on the staff of Magruder at the time of the funeral. It was later recalled that it was a "singular spectacle" that day to observe Federal prisoners of war who had been captured by the Confederacy the day before, who also were Masons, "marching in procession with the brethren, as though for a time a truce had been proclaimed and the clang of arms was to be heard no more."[12]

In the spring of 1863, the U.S. gunboat *Albatross* was anchored in the Mississippi River off Bayou Sara. Lt. Comdr. J. E. Hart, who was in command of the vessel, committed suicide. Hart had been a Mason, and three of his fellow officers on the *Albatross* requested that Confederate W. W. Leake "bury the Captain with Masonic honors." Thus, under a flag of truce, men of the Union vessel, accompanied by Leake and Masonic brothers Capt. Samuel F. White and his sibling Benjamin of Bayou Sara, marched to Grace Church Cemetery, where they "buried Brother Hart in the Masonic lot." The ship surgeon and other Federal officers present cordially invited the Confederates on board the vessel, but the invitation was declined. W. W. Leake later recalled how the Union surgeon "then offered to supply me with necessary family medicines if I would give him a list of what was needed. This I also declined with thanks, but he sent by Brother Samuel White a few medicines. I read the Masonic service at the grave."[13]

Lt. Col. Guy Hulett Watkins, 141st Regiment of Pennsylvania Volunteers, present at the battle of Chancellorsville, was severely wounded by a minié ball in the lung and shoulder blade and left on the battlefield, where he was soon captured by enemy forces. His captors began

> stripping him of his clothing and valuables when on making himself known to the Lieutenant of the company as a Free Mason, he also belonging to the same fraternity, he was sent to the headquarters of General Longstreet, where he was placed under the immediate care of Doctors Guild and Breckenridge, and received the kindest attention.[14]

On August 21, 1993, at Gettysburg, Pennsylvania, a ceremony was held to dedicate the "Friend to Friend—A Brotherhood Undivided" sculpture commemorating an event taking place at that historic site on July 3, 1863, in the battle of Gettysburg. During Pickett's Charge, Confederate brigadier general Lewis A. Armistead and Union major general Winfield S. Hancock were old-time friends, but also Masonic brothers. Both were wounded during the engagement, and as Armistead gave a Masonic cry for assistance, Capt. Henry Bingham, a Union aide to Hancock, came to the mortally wounded Armistead. Bingham was asked by the Rebel general to

"Friend to Friend: A Brotherhood Undivided." Masonic Memorial Monument at Gettysburg. Capt. Henry Bingham (U.S.A.) giving aid to Brig. Gen. Lewis A. Armistead (C.S.A.). COURTESY OF THE NATIONAL PARK SERVICE, GETTYSBURG NATIONAL MILITARY PARK / EISENHOWER NATIONAL HISTORIC SITE.

convey "a message of regret and convey his personal effects, including a Masonic watch, to his old friend Hancock." Armistead died some two days later without seeing Hancock, but "his message was received and the spirit of Brotherhood survived."[15]

Masonic bonds were also demonstrated in prison as well as on the battlefield. Not long after the engagement at Gettysburg, 2nd Lt. Henry Caudill of Co. E, 13th Regiment of Kentucky Cavalry (Confederate), was captured during the battle of Gladesville, Virginia, on July 7, 1863. He and other officers were eventually transported to the famed prison camp located on Johnson's Island in Lake Erie.

Incarcerated for some eleven months and forced out of necessity "to eat rats," he recalled after the war how "he wished he'd been a Mason at the time of his imprisonment." A descendent recalled that "[Caudill] knew of Rebel officers that were Masons at the Prison Camp who received food from the Union guards who were also Masons. He remarked that if he'd been one of them, he would have eaten as they did."[16]

At Waynesboro, Virginia, on September 28, 1864, Capt. George New-man Bliss, Co. B, 1st Rhode Island Cavalry, sustained three saber wounds and was then taken prisoner by the Rebels after his horse was killed. Bliss, having encountered members of the company of Capt. William A. Moss, Buckingham County troops of the 4th Virginia Cavalry, recalls how, during the fight,

> I thought I was safe, when suddenly a bullet, doubtless intended for me, struck my gallant steed and he staggered under the shock. With rein and spur I urged him on, but it was in vain; he fell with a plunge that left me lying upon the ground. Before I could rise two of the enemy reined in their horses by me, and leaning over their saddles struck at me, one with a carbine and the other with a sabre. I could parry but one, and with my sabre stopping the crushing blow from the carbine at the same instant that the sabre gave me a cut across the forehead. I at once rose to my feet and said to the soldier who had wounded me, "For God's sake do not kill a prisoner." "Surrender then," he said; to which I replied, "I do surrender." He demanded my sword and pistol, which I gave him, and had scarcely done so when I was struck on the back with such a force as to thrust me two steps forward.
>
> Upon turning to discover the cause of this assault I found that a soldier had ridden upon the trot and stabbed me with his sabre, which would have passed entirely through my body but for the fact that in his ignorance of the proper use of the weapon he had failed to make the half-turn of the wrist necessary to give the sabre smooth entrance between the ribs. I saw also at this moment another soldier taking aim at me with a revolver.
>
> There was only once chance left me; I called for protection as a Freemason, and Capt. Henry C. Lee, the acting adjutant-general of the enemy's force, at once came to my assistance, ordered a soldier to take me to the rear and see that my wounds were dressed. . . . Later in the evening I was put into an ambulance with Capt. William A. Moss, at that time a lieutenant, and rode several miles

to a small house in the mountains. I found Captain Moss
to be a brother Mason, who did everything possible for
my comfort. He had received a bullet wound from some
other soldier in addition to a sabre-cut from me, but hap-
pily recovered from his wounds and lived many years at
Buckingham Court House, Virginia.[17]

At Rectortown, Virginia, in early November 1864, John S. Mosby's
Rangers had captured twenty-seven Federal soldiers, some of whom he was
determined to execute in retaliation for members of his own command
who had been killed by Federals. On November 6, lots were drawn by the
Union prisoners, seven of whom bore a mark denoting execution. One soldier, Lt. Israel G. Disosway of the 5th New York Heavy Artillery, drew a
fatal lot, and was thus chosen to be killed along with his comrades at a pre-
determined location in the Shenandoah Valley.

On the way to the place of execution, the prisoners and their guards
encountered the flamboyant Confederate captain Richard Montjoy, who
was dressed "with a Masonic pin on the lapel of his coat." Disosway immediately gave the "distress signal to Montjoy," who convinced Edward
Thompson, the ranger in charge of the prisoners, to swap Disosway for another trooper prisoner in his own possession. Disosway was thus released
because of his Masonic connections. Later, when Mosby learned of the exchange, he informed Montjoy that the 43rd Battalion "was no Masonic
Lodge."[18] Nevertheless, the brethren of Freemasonry had once again come
to each other's aid in distress.

At the end of the Civil War, a Confederate soldier lay at the depot in
Danville, Virginia, having been in Richmond convalescing from wounds
received in his side and thigh that had rendered him incapable of walking.
As he waited to go to the hospital, a Federal officer, Lt. Col. Horace Hall
Walpole of the 122nd New York Infantry Regiment, rode by, wearing the
badge of a Mason. The wounded Confederate quickly gave a signal, which
was immediately recognized by Walpole,

who at once alighted, had the poor wounded man removed to the Hospital, giving him such assistance and
kind words as a brother in deed and in fact, only could
give. Yesterday, as the writer of this was returning from
the country he met the wounded Confederate referred to

on a soft bed, half way on his journey to his home in Pitt-
sylvania County. . . .

   We deem comment unnecessary, as such conduct will
always find a proper response in the true brotherhood,
and do more to strengthen the bands of the ancient fraternity than anything we would write.[19]

Fraternizing and fraternal brotherhood partially explain the amiable relations and honorable respect existing at times between the Rebels and
Yankees during the Civil War. The noble virtues of kindness and charity
toward one's enemy, however, were often the sole motives for assistance,
supplanting the desire for trade goods or preexisting oaths of duty and ob-
ligation.

CHAPTER 3

Rebels Aiding Yankees on the Battlefield

WHEN ONE RECALLS FIRST MANASSAS OR THE BATTLE OF BULL RUN OF July 21, 1861, images of renowned officers such as P. G. T. Beauregard, Irvin McDowell, Thomas J. "Stonewall" Jackson, and a host of others come to mind, along with their roles in the famous battle; but stories of atrocities, purportedly committed by Confederate troops upon the Federals, living and dead, began to surface not long after the conflict. As in today's press, sensational accounts sold newspapers and engendered animosity, while occurrences of charity and kindness often went unreported or were not recorded until long after the war.

Confederate colonel Winfield S. Peters, after the war, recalled an event pertaining to Brig. Gen. James R. Herbert, who in 1861 was serving as an officer in the 1st Maryland Infantry Regiment (Confederate). Colonel Peters remarked:

> It was when we were at First Manassas. It was during a lull in the fighting and we were resting on the field. The day was a terribly hot one, and some of our men were engaged in giving water to wounded Federals who lay around. Sitting up against a tree not far off was the captain of a New York company, terribly wounded and dying. He asked to see a Confederate officer. Herbert went to him.

He told Herbert that he knew he was dying, and asked him if he would take his valuables and a message to his wife. The dying officer gave him his watch, money and valuables, and said: "If you survive, I want you to give them to my wife when the war is over."

Herbert carried the trinkets all through the war until he met with his terrible wound at Gettysburg. He was taken to the hospital and there found the wife of the wounded officer whom he saw dying at Manassas, and gave her the trinkets and the dying message. She constantly attended General Herbert until his recovery.[1]

Frank Moore, in his famous postwar collection, *The Civil War in Song and Story,* gives an account of an unnamed Federal soldier from Dodgeville, Wisconsin, serving in the company of Capt. Tom Allen, 2nd Wisconsin Infantry Regiment, who was wounded at the Union disaster of Bull Run, and left along with other Federal Union soldiers on the battlefield. Moore continues the account by stating:

A company of secessionists came where they were lying, and actually bayoneted his wounded companions before his eyes. They even went so far as to stab the bodies of senseless corpses, lest there be some spark of life in them! A man came to where he was lying on the ground and raised his ensanguined weapon for the fatal thrust, which he fully expected would end his mortal career. He closed his eyes, fairly sick with the horrid emotion, and waited to receive his fate.

His enemy hesitated. He lowered his musket, and finally raised him carefully up, and gave him water from his canteen. He was afterwards removed to the hospitals of Richmond, where he received careful treatment, and at last was exchanged and allowed to return home.[2]

J. W. Reid, of the 4th Regiment of South Carolina Volunteers, published a letter he had written in September 1861, concerning his acquisition of two knives picked up from fields of battle. He states that on one of these occasions, he came across a Federal soldier shot through the bowels, whose knife "was laying close to him." He recalled:

> I picked it up and offered it to him. His reply was, "Keep it, friend; I shall need it no more; I am mortally wounded and cannot live to see another sunrise." I gave him a drink of water from my canteen, which I had just filled. . . . He then gave me a package of letters, requesting me to destroy them. I promised to do so and did so. He said that I had given him his last drink of water. Next morning I found him dead, with another letter lying on his breast. I opened and read it, and from the tone of it supposed it to be from his wife; it was at least some female, who advised him to meet her in Heaven, if they never met on earth again. They never met. I hope they may meet in Heaven.
>
> He told me that he was a regular from the State of Maine, but I cannot recollect his name. Could it be possible that my bullet hit him. I hope not, but I fought right in front of where he was. I left him for other scenes equally distresing, and destroyed his last and, I suppose, most cherished letter.[3]

While at the battle of Cheat Mountain in Elkwater, Virginia (now West Virginia), between September 10 and 15, 1861, Lt. Ben R. High of Donelson's Brigade, 8th Tennessee Regiment (C.S.A.) recalled an event "on the third day out." Moving down the hill with Co. E, they "saw a Yank with a broken leg," apparently of the 14th Indiana Regiment, who was placed by other members of the Rebel unit, in a depression where a tree had uprooted, for safety. It was such a lonely place, we could do nothing for him, and I have often wondered about him.[4]

"Bloody Shiloh," or the battle of Pittsburg Landing, fought on April 6–7, 1862, in Tennessee, has a number of humanitarian accounts associated with its events,[5] but perhaps the most dramatic one concerns the experience of Joe T. Williams of Co. D, 21st Alabama Regiment. Having fought the 4th Ohio, he and another comrade came across an eighteen-year-old soldier named John Burns, of Co. B, 4th Ohio, whose cry for water had brought Williams to his side. Burns's "left knee cap was entirely shot off, and he was extremely weak from loss of blood."

Burns had been reading in his Bible, his blood staining the spot. He desired that the testament be sent to his mother, and requested he be taken to a hospital. A Dr. Redwood of the 21st Alabama examined the wounded Federal, but found his injury to be fatal. Upon hearing the news, Williams states the dying Yankee then asked if

> any Christians were present. We told him yes. In the meantime several of our comrades had gathered around him. He requested a prayer, to which one of us responded, all being deeply touched, then repeating a few lines of his mother's favorite song: "There is a land of pure delight, Where saints immortal stand;" which he requested us to sing with him. This song begun there was taken up through the entire camps, even back among the Federal prisoners. All around then bid him good by.
>
> He handed me his Bible and requested me to hand it to Sergeant Stevenson of Company B, Fourth Ohio Regiment. This sergeant knew his family, and he wanted him to send it to his mother and tell her he "died a Christian." The next morning I went to the hospital and learned that he was dead.[6]

At the battle of Williamsburg, Virginia, fought on May 5, 1862, James Burns, serving under Maj. Gen. Daniel E. Sickles, in the 74th New York Infantry or famed 5th Excelsior, was badly wounded in his arm and leg and left exposed upon the battlefield. Confederate soldiers of the "Fifth North Carolina gave him water and one gave him a long drink of thin, but refreshing molasses."[7] This experience is somewhat similar to that of 1st Sgt. Walter W. Carpenter of Co. H, 10th Massachusetts Infantry, "shot through the body just below the left shoulder, the ball passing through his lungs," at the battle of Fair Oaks, Virginia, on May 31, 1862. Left on the field all night, "the rebels used him well—covered him up with a blanket, and gave him water."[8] At the second battle of Bull Run (Manassas) fought August 29–30, 1862, Pvt. James C. Locke of Co. E, 100th Pennsylvania Volunteer Infantry, lost a leg, but a Confederate soldier, "carried him out of the railroad cut in which he lay suffering . . . ministered to his wants as best he could," and before leaving, "provided the suffering Pennsylvanian with a canteen of water."[9] Many years later, after the war, the two former enemies met one another in Kansas City for a happy reunion.

To date, the bloodiest single day in American military history occurred at the battle of Antietam near Sharpsburg, Maryland, on September 17, 1862, where 44,800 men were killed and some 18,500 wounded, of which 5,000 later died. Present at the battle was 1st Sgt. William H. Andrews, of Co. M, 1st Georgia Regulars (C.S.A.). He related the following:

> While I was engaged hunting cartridges, the enemy moved a battery up somewhere in the field in our front and commenced shelling the woods, several bursting near me. I saw not far from me a wounded yankee. He was sitting on the ground with his back to a tree. He had been shot through the thigh. As I got within 15 feet of him a shell burst between us. I dodged . . . walked up and squatted down by him. He had his pants ripped up to where he was shot, and was bathing his wound with water from his canteen. . . .
>
> He then told me he was the color bearer of the 1st Minn. Regiment, carried the colors at First Manassas, and had been carrying them ever since. But said he, "Some of you boys have been too sharp for me this morning."
>
> Wondered to myself if he was the color bearer I was so anxious to shoot in the first of the fight. *Have no desire to harm him now. He is wounded and would do anything in my power to aid or assist him.* Strange that while he was on his feet I would have killed him if I could, but now he is down at my mercy, have no animosity towards him.[10]

After the war, Samuel Bloomer related his own version of that memorable day at Antietam, stating how a Confederate soldier, the aforementioned W. H. Andrews, of the 1st Georgia Regulars,

> came up, learning my condition and the fact that I was between two fires, he and some of his comrades piled cord wood around me to protect me from the shots. I have no doubt that more than a hundred bullets struck that barricade during the day.
>
> Early in the morning Stonewall Jackson came riding by. He halted a moment, spoke kindly to me, asked to what regiment I belonged, and ordered the men who had

charge of a lot of Union prisoners to supply my wants and make me as comfortable as possible.

A Captain of a North Carolina regiment a little later stopped and chatted with me, gave me a drink from his canteen, and spoke kindly and encouragingly. He rode away, but returned during the night and replenished my canteen with cool water.[11]

Color Sergeant Bloomer lay on the battlefield until the evening of the next day, "when the Confederates carried him on a stretcher to a little barn," where other Union prisoners had also been taken. Not long after, his leg was amputated by Asst. Surg. Edmund J. Pugsley of the 1st Minnesota, and he was discharged from military service.[12]

During the battle of Shepherdstown Bluff, West Virginia, fought on September 20, 1862, Pvt. George D. Canon, a native of Philadelphia and member of Co. K, 118th Pennsylvania Infantry, was wounded. Three balls had passed through his body, inflicting severe wounds through his right arm and shoulder, one embedding itself in his left shoulder, "whence it was dug out by a Rebel surgeon."

According to the newspaper account that recorded the incident, Private Canon

fell forward, while Jackson's force charged over him and down the bluff. . . . While lying there he could distinctly feel the heat from the shells of our artillery on the left bank of the Potomac, as they passed over him.

Twice he heard the voice and could partly see the body of a Rebel soldier coming up as far as safety would permit, calling to him to "come down from there or you will be killed." "I cannot," said George, "I am wounded." The Rebel, at the risk of his own life, and to save the wounded man from the shells intended to carry death among his own comrades, ascended the bank, raised the Union soldier on his feet, kindly bid him look after his blanket, and supported him down the hill, where, with other Union prisoners, he was led out of danger.[13]

George D. Canon was confined in the Rebel hospital at Shepherdstown, then transferred to the hospital care of Virginia Unionists. He eventually arrived home in Philadelphia, but died on October 27, 1862, from wounds he had received during the aforementioned battle.[14]

That same year, on October 4, W. A. Anderson of Co. A, 15th Arkansas Infantry, was fighting in the battle of Corinth, in Mississippi. It was during this engagement that Anderson recalled how he "found an Irish Federal soldier wounded on the field, his left thigh being broken." With a pocketknife he "removed the bullet, and with the assistance of a comrade carried him to the hospital."[15]

One of the most well-known accounts of human compassion and selfless sacrifice exhibited during the Civil War took place on the hill known as Marye's Heights, near Fredericksburg, Virginia, during the battle fought there from December 11 to 13, 1862. As the Federal forces attempted to scale the heights, Confederate batteries and musketry claimed a horrendous toll. In some cases the dead were piled three deep. It is here that Gen. Robert E. Lee is said to have made his famous remark: "It is well that war is so terrible, else we would grow fond of it."

Witnessing the slaughter of the Union forces was a young nineteen-year-old Rebel sergeant named Richard Rowland Kirkland from Kershaw County, South Carolina, serving in Co. B, of the 2nd South Carolina Volunteer Infantry. By sunset of the battle's first day, some 12,000 Federal troops lay dead or dying upon the slopes of Marye's Heights, and as night fell, their cries and moans of pain and thirst began to be heard in great numbers.

On December 13 the unearthly cries of distress could still be heard through the fog blanketing the site. Finally, Sergeant Kirkland could stand it no longer, and leaving the stone wall where the Southern troops had carried out their "shower of death," went to see his commander, Gen. J. B. Kershaw, who wrote an account of their conversation in the *Charleston News and Courier*, on February 6, 1880. He recalled:

> Kirkland came up. With an expression of indignant demonstrance pervading his person, his manner and the tenor of his voice, he said:
>> General, I can't stand this.
> "What is the matter, sergeant?" asked the general.
> He replied:
>> All night and all day I have heard those poor people crying for water, and I can stand it no

Richard Rowland Kirkland, Co. B, 2nd South Carolina Infantry (C.S.A.), or "The Angel of Marye's Heights."
COURTESY OF SOUTH CAROLINIANA LIBRARY, UNIVERSITY OF SOUTH CAROLINA, COLUMBIA.

longer. I came to ask permission to go and give them water.

The general regarded him for a moment with feelings of profound admiration and said:

Kirkland, don't you know that you would get a bullet through your head the moment you stepped over the wall?

"Yes, sir," he said, "I know all about that, but if you will let me, I am willing to try it."

After a pause, the general said:

Kirkland, I ought not to allow you to run such a risk, but the sentiment which actuates you is so noble, that I will not refuse your request, trusting that God may protect you. You may go.

The sergeant's eyes lighted up with pleasure. He said, "Thank you, sir" and ran rapidly down stairs. The general

heard him pause a moment and then return, bounding
two steps at a time.

He thought the sergeant's heart had failed him. He was
mistaken.

The sergeant stopped at the door and said:

General, can I show a white handkerchief?

The general slowly shook his head, saying emphatically:

No, Kirkland, you can't do that.

"All right, sir," he said, "I'll take the chances."[16]

Securing some dozen canteens or more, Kirkland soon amazed thousands of men on both sides, as he climbed the wall and began carrying out
his errand of mercy. At first the Union forces believed he was attempting
"to rob the dead and wounded," and thus began shooting at the "Good
Samaritan" soldier. Soon, however, his true motives were discovered and his
actions were admired and cheered by the enemy and his fellow Confederates. For more than an hour and a half, Kirkland brought relief to the pros-
trate foe.[17] The "Angel of Marye's Heights" soon became a legend in both
armies, and today a bronze monument stands in front of the stone wall at
Fredericksburg, Virginia, depicting him lifting the head of a wounded
Union soldier, to give a drink of refreshing water.

Richard Rowland Kirkland would continue to fight for a time in the
Civil War, at Gettysburg, and finally at the battle of Chickamauga, in
Georgia, where on September 20, 1863, he was shot in the chest. Two of
his companions, Ario Niles and James W. Arrants, bore him off the battlefield. With blood pouring from his mouth, he is said to have gasped his
last words, stating, "I am done for. You can do me no good. Save yourselves
and tell my Pa I died right."[18]

As the war dragged on through 1863, examples of mercy service or humanitarian aid by Confederate troops toward their Northern enemies did
not decrease. Mrs. Frank Townsend Dade, wife of a Union army physician
stationed at Beaufort, South Carolina, wrote home in April to her sisters in
Philadelphia concerning an attack by the Rebels on a Federal gunboat "at
the Ferry." She remarked how the Confederates

fired two shots—the second took effect in the powder
magazine and blew the whole concern up—a good many
were badly wounded—some saved themselves by jumping
into the water and swam to shore—The Officers all made

Monument of Richard Rowland Kirkland, Spotsylvania National Military Park, Fredericksburg, Virginia. COURTESY OF THE NATIONAL PARK SERVICE.

their escape and left the poor fellows at the mercy of the Rebels. They are very much censured.

The Rebels came over and took care of our wounded. Then sent them over under a Flag of Truce. The men say they were very kind to them.[19]

The battle of Gettysburg, Pennsylvania, July 1–3, 1863, has been the topic of numerous monographs, articles, and a recent movie, and continues to be one of the most popular historical sites visited each year in the United States. It is thus not too surprising to learn that during this great decisive battle of the Civil War, soldiers performed acts of mercy toward one another, even during the heat of the action.

A private of Co. E, 153rd Pennsylvania Regiment, lying wounded on the field at Gettysburg, feared that he might possibly be shot by his own comrades. As Levi F. Walter stated, "[That] this did not occur was entirely owing to the kind services of a Confederate soldier." Walter recalled that

[n]earby there was a clump of large trees. . . . Now in the enemy's line, formed in the rear, was one particular Rebel

who took advantage of the protection afforded by these trees. As the balls from our own Union forces were flying fast around him, the writer asked the Rebel to place a large, loose tree stump that lay a short distance away, in front of him. "I don't like the idea of being hit by my own regiment," he said.

Hardly had the Rebel gotten back behind his own tree when three minie balls struck the stump in front of the writer. "Young man, I saved your life," called the Rebel. The aforesaid young man was not scant in his thanks, as may well be imagined.[20]

Present at the battle of Gettysburg was Maj. Israel Putnam Spaulding of the 141st Regiment of Pennsylvania Volunteers. He was twice wounded, one ball striking a thigh, and another breaking his ankle as an attempt was made to carry him off the field. Left in the hands of the enemy, he lay all night amid the numerous dead, entirely helpless because of his wounds. The next day, however, he was removed from the field by orders of Brig. Gen. Benjamin G. Humphreys of the Confederate Brigade composed of the 13th, 17th, 18th, and 21st Mississippi Infantry Regiments. Spaulding was "carried to the rear where a surgeon dressed his wounds and set a pail of water to keep the bandages wet. The soldiers of the enemy treated him very kindly."[21] Major Spaulding's leg had to be amputated, however, and he died on July 28 as a result of the wounds received at Gettysburg.

Another Union casualty, Pvt. John B. Stowe of the 9th Massachusetts Battery, was wounded on July 2 during the battle. He later remembered that he "was shot through the body . . . went to the rear about twenty yards and fell senseless." His fellow soldiers were forced to leave him since the Rebel lines were advancing. He lay in this painful condition, watching the enemy establish a picket line. Stowe recalled:

> The night was long and dark to me; I thought if the boys could they would come for me. Toward morning a man in gray came near me. He appeared to be looking about, but not trying to strip any bodies. He stood looking at me, and I put out my hand and touched his foot; he jumped as if surprised; he probably thought me dead.

On recovering, he stooped down, asked me where I was shot, if I was cold, and got a rubber blanket and got it under me, and covered me with two of woolen. He sat by me some time talking, till it began to be light, then gave me his canteen of water, saying he must get back to his post.[22]

One widely published and well-known incident is attributed to a Federal soldier about his contact with Gen. Robert E. Lee at Gettysburg, as related by Brig. Gen. A. L. Long of the Confederacy and Brig. Gen. Marcus J. Wright of the Federal army. The soldier is purported to have remarked:

> I was at the battle of Gettysburg myself, and an incident occurred there which largely changed my views of the Southern people. I had been a most bitter anti-South man, and fought and cursed the Confederacy desperately. I could see nothing good in any of them. The last day of the fight I was badly wounded. A ball shattered my left leg. I lay on the ground not far from Cemetery Ridge, and as General Lee ordered his retreat he and his officers rode near me.
>
> As they came along I recognized him, and, though faint from exposure and loss of blood, I raised up my hands, looked Lee in the face, and shouted as loud as I could, "Hurrah for the Union!" The general heard me, looked, stopped his horse, dismounted, and came toward me. I confess that I at first thought he meant to kill me.
>
> But as he came up he looked down at me with such a sad expression upon his face that all fear left me, and I wondered what he was about. He extended his hand to me, and grasping mine firmly and looking right into my eyes, said, "My son, I hope you will soon be well."
>
> If I live a thousand years I shall never forget the expression on General Lee's face. There he was, defeated, retiring from a field that had cost him and his cause almost their last hope, and yet he stopped to say words like those to a wounded soldier of the opposition who had taunted him

as he passed by! As soon as the general had left me I cried myself to sleep there upon the bloody ground.[23]

A frequently told story of Gettysburg was first brought to light in the reminiscences of Confederate general John Brown Gordon, formerly of the 6th Alabama Regiment, who by July 1863 had become a commander of an entire Georgia brigade. Maj. Gen. Jubal A. Early of the Confederacy, in his official report of the Gettysburg campaign, remarked how Gordon "succeeded in routing the force opposed to him, consisting of a division of the Eleventh Corps, commanded by Brigadier-General Barlow, of the Federal Army, and drove it back with great slaughter, capturing, among a number of prisoners, General Barlow himself, who was severely wounded."[24] Gordon's own report remarks that he had indeed taken prisoners, and that among the latter "was a division commander (General [F. C.] Barlow) who was severely wounded."[25]

Though the veracity of the following account has been called into question in recent years, no significant proof has come forth to dispel this incident as a work of fiction.[26] According to General Gordon's postwar account, he came across the wounded body of Maj. Gen. Francis Channing Barlow of New York, whose "life seemed to be rapidly ebbing out." The Union officer was shot by a minié ball that had passed out close to the spine, thus paralyzing both his arms and legs. Gordon states:

> Quickly dismounting and lifting his head, I gave him water from my canteen. . . . Neither of us had the remotest thought that [Barlow] could possibly survive many hours. I summoned several soldiers who were looking after the wounded, and directed them to place him upon a litter and carry him to the shade in the rear. Before parting he asked me to take from his pocket a package of letters and destroy them. They were from his wife. He had but one request to make of me . . . that if I should live to the end of the war and should ever meet Mrs. Barlow, I would tell her of our meeting on the field of Gettysburg and of his thoughts of her in his last moments.
>
> I learned that Mrs. Barlow was with the Union Army, and near the battle-field. . . . Passing through the day's battle unhurt, I despatched at its close, under flag of truce,

the promised message to Mrs. Barlow. . . . In the desperate encounters of the two succeeding days, and the retreat of Lee's army, I thought no more of Barlow, except to number him with the noble dead of the two armies.[27]

According to Gordon, both he and Barlow went through the war believing that the other had been killed during the conflict, Barlow not realizing that the J. B. Gordon, of whose death he learned, merely shared the last name and initials of the general who aided him at Gettysburg. Later, however, the men met one another in New York and had a surprising reunion, becoming fast friends for life.[28]

On August 22, 1893, Thomas S. Kenan of Raleigh, North Carolina, formerly colonel of the Confederate 43rd North Carolina Infantry, addressed a letter to John B. Callis of Lancaster, Wisconsin. Callis had served originally as a lieutenant colonel of the 7th Wisconsin Infantry during the battle of Gettysburg. According to Kenan:

After the engagement had continued for some time the Union forces fell back and occupied Seminary Ridge, and later in the afternoon this became the point of attack by the Confederates. . . . The firing having ceased . . . Lieutenant Shepherd, of my regiment, reported to me that among the wounded in our front was Lieutenant-Colonel Callis, of the Seventh Wisconsin, and that he (or his father's family) was from Fayetteville, N.C., Shepherd himself being also a Fayetteville man. . . . Thereupon I went forward and found him lying a little beyond the crest of the ridge. . . .

I well remember telling you that "You are now my prisoner, and I'll treat you well; I may be yours later on." And so it happened, for I was wounded on Culp's Hill on 3 July, taken off the field, placed in an ambulance and captured on the retreat on the night of 4 July, with many other wounded Confederates, and was a prisoner until the war closed.

I hope we will meet at Gettysburg again, not on a hostile, but on a friendly historic field, when our performances will be impressed with a character different from that of 1863.

On September 3, 1893, Colonel Callis replied to the letter written by his former foe, aptly substantiating Kenan's reminiscences. He related how he still carried "a souvenir in the shape of a minie ball" in his right lung from the Gettysburg engagement, though over thirty years had transpired. He remarked:

> I have always admired a gentleman who never forgets that he is a gentleman no matter what his environs may be, and must say that I took you to be such, when you kindly treated me as your prisoner of war on the field at Gettysburg, hence the presentation of my spurs, I thinking I would have no more use for them. . . . The facts were so indelibly fixed on my mind that they are as fresh to me as though they were of yesterday, and are as follows:
>
> On the morning of 1 July 1863, about 9:30 o'clock, the Iron Brigade, composed of the Second, Sixth and Seventh Wisconsin, Nineteenth Indiana and Twenty-fourth Michigan, charged General Archer's Brigade. . . . In this charge my horse was killed and I was slightly wounded, and not taking time to shed my spurs, I went in on foot. . . . Most of our field officers, having been wounded or killed in the morning, what was left of our brigade was in a tight place. We moved by the right of companies to the rear, making the Seminary on the Ridge our objective point. Being closely pursued by the Confederates, we faced, wheeled into line and fired. . . .
>
> Many a brave North Carolinian bit the dust in that movement before we reached the Seminary. At this juncture I was shot in the right breast, the ball entering my lung, where it still remains. . . . The first thing I remember, I was surrounded by private Confederate soldiers, who were curiously examining my uniform, they taking my coat off, in the side pocket of which was my pocketbook containing $220 in greenbacks and gold, with papers by which I might be identified should I be found dead on the field.
>
> They went and sat down on the railroad grade near by and were examining the contents of the pocketbook

when an officer came to me and saw my condition. He interrogated me as to my rank, regiment, name and nativity, and in stooping over me to catch my words I thought I could see signs of pity depicted on his face, which gave me hope. I asked him to unbuckle the spur from my boot. He did so and seeing the other foot bootless, he asked its meaning. I told him some of the men had pulled it off without unbuckling the spur and that it nearly tore the leg off.

He looked around and found the boot with the spur on it; he took it off and threw the boots and spurs by my side, asking at the same time if they had taken anything else from me. I told them [the gathered Confederate soldiers] they had taken my coat and money. He inquired who they were, and I, pointing to them on the railroad grade, said, "There they are now." He looked and saw them and ordered them to restore the pocketbook and money, which they did—he placing the book and money in an inside pocket of my coat. I told him to take the money and send it to my family, as I feared it would be an incentive for the men to finish me and take the money as soon as his back was turned on me. He replied, "I will see that you are taken care of," and I soon found myself in charge of two Confederates, one a German and one an Irishman, with a negro to bring water and pour on my wounds, and faithfully too, they did their whole duty. . . .

I have told the story of the spurs and your kindness until it has become a "campfire story" all over the State, and told it as I relate it to you; and I wish there were more frequently such interchange of friendly greetings between ex-Confederate and Union soldiers as this between you and me.[29]

Colonel Callis was born in Fayetteville, North Carolina, but his family had moved to Tennessee, and finally to Lancaster in Grant County, Wisconsin, while it was still a territory. Ill health prevented Callis from ever meeting Kenan at Gettysburg; he died in the year 1897.

Two months after Gettysburg, on September 19, at the battle of Chickamauga in Georgia, Frederick J. Haller of Co. A, 101st Ohio Infantry, was shot by a ball below his left eye, which passed quickly through his head and out the back of his neck. He lay through the night on the field in an unconscious condition, but in the morning a "rebel soldier gave him a drink . . . and covered him with a tent cloth."[30]

A Union private of Co. K, 93rd Ohio Infantry, had his leg broken by a musket ball near Jay's Mill. Unable to leave, William C. Brown later encountered that evening a squad of five Confederates to whom he called out for assistance. He stated:

> They halted, and asked who I was and what I wanted. I replied that I was a wounded Federal soldier, and wanted to be helped into an easier position, as I was suffering from a broken leg. They came to me promptly and assisted me[,] as gently as if I had been one of their own men or a brother[,] to a large tree, where I would be protected from the fire of our own men, first taking off my woolen blanket and spreading it down for me to lie on, placing my cartridge box under my head for a pillow and spreading my oilcloth over me.
>
> The tenderness with which they had lifted me touched me, and I said: "Boys, an hour or two ago we were engaged in shooting each other, and now you are treating me with the greatest kindness. I hardly know how to thank you for it in return." They only replied, "Well, old fellow, we are doing to you only as we should like to be done by. It may come our turn next." [A]nd they passed on to the front picket line for the night. . . . The next morning, when I awoke . . . I found that one of them had spread half of a homemade calico quilt over me, saying nothing about it, and doubtless keeping the other half to shelter him in his nightlong watch on picket post.
>
> Was there ever a more beautiful type of chivalry and Christian charity than this?[31]

A participant in the engagement at Rogersville, Tennessee, fought on November 6, 1863, Capt. Theodore F. Allen of the 7th Ohio Cavalry recalled after the war the events of the battle. While under fire his horse had stumbled, causing him to fall and lie unconscious for a time. Allen wrote:

> I do not know how long I lay on the field; but with the return of consciousness the first thing I knew was that a Confederate soldier was trying to take my boots off. . . . After I had convinced this soldier that the time had not yet come to number me among the dead, he gave me a helping hand and assisted me to a log cabin near by. Here he supplied me with water taken from a well. . . .
>
> This soldier helped me to bathe my face and remove the blood and mud from my face and hair. . . . The soldier was a member of the Fourth Kentucky Confederate Cavalry.[32]

Allen further remarked how he and other Union soldiers were made prisoners, and while marching toward Libby Prison and Belle Isle, they were

> turned into a large meadow with a heavy guard around us. Neither the Confederate soldiers or the prisoners had anything to eat.
>
> I remember making an appeal to a Confederate officer for some food. He told me that all he had to eat was two apples, but that he would be very glad to divide with me, which he did, giving me one apple and keeping one himself.[33]

On May 5, 1864, during the battle of the Wilderness in Virginia, 4th Sgt. William H. Tondee of Co. B, 17th Georgia Infantry, encountered a wounded Federal soldier who had been "shot in the thigh, and asked the aid of some one to get in an upright position behind a tree, as he was in danger of shots from his own men." Tondee remarks, "I gave him the required assistance."[34]

During the same battle, Luther W. Hopkins, of J. E. B. Stuart's Confederate Cavalry, Co. A, 6th Virginia Regiment, recalled coming across "two Yankees lying mortally wounded." A short conversation ensued, one soldier bearing a picture of his sister on his person. Both had been shot in the breast and were bleeding profusely. Hopkins states that it "was very evident that they had but a short time to live. The Captain ordered them to be taken back to a place of safety."[35]

A "Petersburg Rifleman," George S. Bernard of Co. E, 12th Virginia Infantry, William Mahone's Brigade, C.S.A., related that at the battle of the Wilderness, he and other members of his company moved through the woods

> in pursuit of the retreating Federals. . . . I think three [. . .] of us fired simultaneously at one retreating Federal. . . . As we fired, the Federal soldier fell. Leroy Edwards, who was at my side, and one of those who fired, exclaimed, "I hit him!" . . . In a few seconds we were at his side and to our surprise he did not appear to be badly hurt. Leroy Edwards, as tender-hearted as he was courageous, first spoke to him, and offering to help, or helping him, to get to his feet, said in the most sympathetic way, "I hope you are not hurt!"
>
> This striking incident, illustrating the feeling of a true and chivalrous soldier towards his fallen enemy, impressed me very much.[36]

A soldier who served in Co. G, of the 10th Massachusetts Infantry Regiment, recalled in 1872 his experience at the battle of Spotsylvania, Virginia, fought on May 12, 1864. A ball passed through his right foot and Francis Williams was soon taken into the Rebel lines, where he was retained for some twenty-four hours. He wrote:

> Our men then sent in a flag of truce, and stood in arms with their hands up for the purpose of giving us a chance to escape from the terrible position in which we were then placed, it being under the muzzles of the rebel guns. . . . One of our men told me they had ceased firing, and had better try and get out of there. The rebels seeing I could not go, kindly helped me to a place of safety. . . .
>
> I asked for water; they said they had none for themselves, but they gave me some corn-cake. It had been raining all night, and there were about six inches of water

in the trench. I lay there all night. . . . I inquired if he could not get me a piece of tent, or something, to put under my head. He said . . . "As soon as your men stop firing I will help you a little." Soon after the whole body of rebels moved off, and I was alone with the dead and wounded. As soon as I could see in the morning, with the assistance of two men, I got back to our lines.[37]

A member of the 61st Georgia Infantry, Pvt. G. W. Nichols, described the battles of Winchester and Fisher's Hill in Virginia, fought on September 19 and 22, respectively, in 1864. He stated that the topography of the area was quite "hilly," and he "went to the line of dead and wounded Yankees," where he heard

. . . lamentations and cries for water. Many of them were in a few feet of nice spring water, but were unable to get it. They called me and said, "Johnny Reb, for God's sake give me some water," or, "Do, Johnny, give me some water." I had the pleasure of devoting about thirty minutes to giving those wounded Yankees water. I would fill their canteens with water and give it to them. Several died while I was there. Our litter corps came to their assistance.[38]

Not only Confederate Rebels practiced kindness and charity upon the battlefield. The following chapter will reveal that the Federal Union forces, as well, were instrumental in caring for their ailing foes upon the field.

CHAPTER 4

Yankees Aiding Rebels

GEORGE HAY STUART, A SUPPORTER DURING THE CIVIL WAR OF THE humanitarian organization known as the U.S. Christian Commission, in speaking of the Rebels found upon a battlefield at Martinsburg, Virginia, said:

> If we found them dying, we took their last messages and wrote to their friends, just as if they had been our own soldiers. It was the same in the hospitals. The poor fellows would sometimes burst into tears. One of them said, "You fight us like devils, but nurse us like angels."[1]

This tribute was often paid to the regular Federal troops by the common Confederate soldier as well. One Yankee recalled an incident occurring in the mountains of East Tennessee, where he was approached by a half-frozen Rebel while performing picket duty. As the Confederates were always destitute for adequate supplies, it is little wonder that the Rebel remarked: "My uniform's nothing but rags, and I haven't got any overcoat or blanket or anything. Blankets are scarce over in our camp, and it's awful cold, Yank."

The Northerner graciously "got half a dozen blankets out of the commissary" and brought them to the Rebel the next night. In speaking of this event, the Federal soldier commented about how the Rebel

> fell down on his knees (I could see him in the dim moonlight), and I never heard anybody pray such a prayer as the Southern soldier prayed for me, kneeling there in the snow in his ragged old uniform. I took off my hat and stood still till he was through, and then he faded away in the darkness.[2]

A member of Co. H, of the 4th Alabama (C.S.A.), was wounded at First Manassas or Bull Run in 1861, "shot through the lungs and . . . left among the killed and wounded." Shortly thereafter, a "Yankee" soldier came to James Jackson's side and stated, "Friend, you appear to be badly wounded, what can I do for you?" Jackson replied, "Some water, for God's sake." In giving him the water the Federal noticed the "fob chain" of Jackson's watch, hooked in his vest, and promised to take it to his mother since it appeared he would not live much longer. Jackson stated, "If you will place me in the shade, and fill my canteen with water, I will give you the watch." The "trade" was carried out, but Jackson failed to die, and recovered to tell the tale.[3]

At Gauley Bridge, [now West] Virginia, prior to the battle fought there November 1–3, 1861, Steward D. Painter of Co. B, 45th Virginia Infantry, "was shot through the left lung, near the heart," and fell into the hands of the Federal forces. A Dr. Henry Z. Gill, assistant surgeon of the 11th Ohio Infantry Regiment, commented about how "the wounded man was greatly exhausted from loss of blood, and somewhat frightened to find himself in the hands of the terrible 'yankees.'" He was taken by the surgeon to a local resident's home where he began to recover.

Painter wrote a letter of appreciation to Dr. Gill on November 4, 1861:

> I write this for the purpose of expressing in written language my gratitude to you for the generous, kindly treatment you bestowed on me, who your enemy, rendered unfortunate by the fate of war, was thrown upon your

mercy. Sir, it is impossible for me to express all that my
heart dictates. Suffice it to say that I can never forget you.
. . . May heaven smile upon you Doctor; may your path
be strewn with life's choicest flowers; may you pass un-
scathed through the horrors of this unnatural war, and
when you die may these words be your stay and support—"Inasmuch as ye did it unto the least of these, ye
did it unto me."[4]

In his report of the engagement at Belmont, Missouri, which transpired on November 7, 1861, Col. Henry Dougherty, of the 22nd Illinois
Infantry, remarked how soldiers of the 2nd Brigade advanced,

pressing on over the enemy's dead and wounded, many of
whom implored our men not to murder them, being evidently under the belief of the false and wicked impression
so industriously sought to be made by many of the leaders of this cursed rebellion that we were barbarians and
savages, but instead of murdering them some of our men
ministered to their wants and conveyed them to places of
safety.[5]

After the war, a veteran of the 11th Connecticut, W. B. Lowell, told of
the battle of New Bern, North Carolina (March 14, 1862). He and his
comrades came on the body of Confederate artillery officer Capt. James H.
Mayo of the North Carolina 2nd Artillery, who had been thrown over 100
feet after blowing up his own magazine as the Federal troops were attack-
ing. Lowell related the details:

About night in going through some thick brush we found,
lying on the ground on an old army blanket in which his
men had dragged him from the field, this young man;
face, neck and hands burned black and badly torn, his
eyes seemed burned out, and blood trickling from his
whole body which was swollen—in fact, he was the worst
looking object to be alive I ever saw. Really, I could not
realize that he was alive until I asked his men . . . who told
us they had come back to look for him after the explosion.

I asked: "Who is this?" "Capt. Mayo." "How was he killed? The Captain then spoke: "I am not quite dead. . . . A little water, if you please, if you have it: you will have to pour it into my mouth, as I can't see nor use my hands." I did as he requested, which seemed to revive him, and he thanked me.

Captain Mayo was soon taken by stretcher and attended by Union surgeon Dr. James B. Whitcomb of the 11th Connecticut. While convalescing, Lowell read books to the Rebel officer and played "the violin for him." Through the kind ministration of the Federal medical corps, Captain Mayo regained his eyesight and was able in some five months to ride in an ambulance. He and his men were sent by General Burnside "through the lines without paroling them."[6]

In his reminiscences after the war, James Grant of the U.S. Christian Commission recalled an incident related to him by George R. Sheffield, of Co. I, 44th New York Volunteers, who had been wounded previously at the battle of Hanover Courthouse, Virginia, fought on May 27, 1862. While removing the wounded soldier's coat to replace his blood-saturated shirt with a clean one, Grant felt "a small book in the pocket." He relates:

I took it out, and found it was a Testament. On opening it to ascertain his name I noticed written on the fly leaf, "I. M. Jones 18th North Carolina Vols." "Why," said I, "this is not your name" (for he was a Union soldier). "How did you get it?" He replied, "It was a gift from a rebel soldier," and stated that he was formerly wounded at the battle of Hanover Court House and that close to where he lay on the field was a Confederate very severely wounded crying piteously for water: "he longed so for it that I crawled to a stream near by, filled my canteen, and held it to his mouth while he drank it greedily."

The poor fellow wanted to shew [*sic*] me his gratitude, so he handed me his little Testament saying it was all he could do and was "the most precious thing he could give me." An hour afterwards he was silent, painless, and thirstless, in death.[7]

A corporal with the 5th Regiment of New Hampshire Volunteer Infantry, Charles A. Hale, related that during the battle of Antietam, fought on September 17, 1862, as he and his comrades fell back over fences,

> [t]he dead and wounded were literally piled in there in heaps. As we went over them in crossing the road, a wounded reb made a thrust at me with his bayonet; turning my head to look at him I saw that he was badly hurt, and kept on.

Later during the same battle, Corporal Hale saw the same wounded rebel and stated, "I thought of that bayonet thrust, but my reb was not so pugnacious this time, though I saw him glaring at me as I picked my way over the heaps." The 5th New Hampshire soon retreated back the way they had come, and Hale once again encountered his counterpart in gray. He recalled:

> I started back towards the regiment on the run. Reaching the sunken road there was that Johnny right before me, but he had lost all his animosity. "Say, Yank, for the love of God lift that dead man off 'n my hurt leg." With the butt of my rifle for a lever I thrust the dead body away from his legs and went on.[8]

James Grant, in his reminiscences of work with the U.S. Christian Commission, also mentions that at Antietam disabled Union soldiers were taken to a nearby farmhouse in the vicinity, which overlooked the battle site:

> Our own supplies were at once exhausted, the stock of clothing being reduced to a single shirt. Looking around to discover the most needy, I observed an elderly soldier of a New York regiment, leaning against the barn-door. He was severely wounded in the breast, and appeared weak from the loss of blood. He had no shirt, but had substituted for it a few blood-soaked, weather-hardened fragments of an outer coat.

"You are the very man I am looking for," said I, "nobody could need this 'last shirt' more than you."

His reply thrilled me: "I'm much obleeged t'ye, sir, but,—"and he pointed to a spot on the hill-side near by, "down yonder there's a poor 'Johnny' far worse off nor I am, an' av ye'll plaze t' give 't till me, I'll put it on him by-and-bye."

I handed him the shirt, and its benevolent errand was soon accomplished.[9]

Rebel sergeant George S. Bernard, who served in Co. I, "Meherrin Breys," of the 12th Virginia Regiment in Gen. William Mahone's Brigade, was wounded and captured during the battle of Crampton's Gap, fought in Maryland on September 14, 1862. A wounded comrade was Lt. J. Richard Manson, who lay next to Bernard on the battlefield, and who

repeatedly called out to the Federals over the fence to "be cautious and not shoot us, that we were wounded men," and that we had "surrendered," of which they took no notice, until, placing the white pocket-handkerchief I took from my leg upon the end of a ramrod, he held it up almost in their faces, at the same time saying to them, "We surrender! We are wounded men!" whereupon one or two of them said, "Get over the fence, then—get over the fence," at which Lieut. Hanson, who was a strong, athletic man, seizing me in his arms, lifted me up to the top of the fence and with the assistance of one of the Federals tumbled me over to the other side, and then bore me in his arms across the ploughed field to the Federal rear. . . .

Two Federal soldiers came up and kindly assisted Lieut. Hanson in bearing me at least a mile back to a house at which the Federal surgeons had improvised a hospital. . . . One of the Federal soldiers who helped to bear me to the field-hospital told me his name was Ellsworth, that he was a relative of Col. Ellsworth, of the Zouaves, who was killed by Jackson in the historic Mansion House trajedy [*sic*] at Alexandria in May, 1861. . . . His treatment of me was kind and considerate, and he was manifestly a manly fellow. . . .

As I was about to be placed on the grass along with the other wounded men, a middle-aged gentleman, of kindly and sympathetic manner, came up and remarking that no distinction would be made between the wounded men, whether Federal or Confederate, asked me how I felt, and what he could do for me. At the same time he said that he was the chaplain of a Maine regiment. I told him I felt very weak, and that I thought a drink of some stimulant would help me. . . . He disappeared from my side, and in a little while returned with some tea in a tin cup, which I drank with great relish and benefit. . . .

Soon after . . . I was carried into the house and a Federal surgeon and nurse came to dress my wound.[10]

A cavalry officer of the Army of Northern Virginia, Thomas T. Munford, was wounded during the Crampton's Gap conflict, and had his arm broken by a bullet that left it useless. Taking shelter in an old cooper shop, he encountered a number of Federal soldiers "making good use of several barrels of fresh cider." He remembered:

I passed by them, and seated myself on the back sill, feeling quite faint from the loss of blood.

I was not there more than a minute when one of the number brought me a tin cup of the cider, addressing me as "Johnnie." He seemed very much interested in my condition, and insisted on going with me to have my wound attended to. I was utterly amazed at this mark of kindness, and I soon followed him over the field. . . .

About midway my eyes rested on the finest canteen I had ever seen, and I hardly thought it would be violating the Tenth Commandment if I asked him to appropriate it for my use, and this he did most cheerfully.

I was taken to five operating "field" hospitals before a surgeon could be found. . . . In an apple orchard, near a brick house, about one mile in the rear of the battlefield,

Gen. Thomas T. Munford, Army of Northern Virginia. Courtesy of The Historical Society of Pennsylvania, Philadelphia.

a very noble and kindly disposed Federal surgeon, about sixty years old, with a sharp knife ripped my sleeve open, and cut it off about two inches below the shoulder. . . . An incision about two inches long was made through the ligaments, and fastening the forceps on the bullet, they failed to remove it, until the fourth or fifth effort. When it yielded . . . the blood flew in all directions. He crammed a bunch of lint into the opening. The next minute everything turned pitch dark and I lost consciousness for several minutes.

When I recovered, this kind doctor was bathing my face in cool water, and had such a sympathetic countenance that I felt he was a friend. . . .

The Union soldier who accompanied me from the battlefield had remained by me, and as it was about sundown he brought me a small bowl of corn meal gruel, which refreshed me very much. . . .

I laid on the upper porch floor of the brick house that night, on a bed of loose straw, brought by this kind Federal soldier, who also brought a canteen of fresh water, which proved a great blessing, for my thirst was insatiate, and I could not sleep. On the same porch floor with me were six or seven wounded Federal soldiers, two of whom died before daybreak.

Next morning my soldier friend brought me another bowl of gruel and a cup of coffee.[11]

Medals of honor were actually given to four Federal soldiers of Co. A, 66th Ohio Infantry, for aiding and "succoring the enemy" at the battle of Chancellorsville, Virginia, fought May 1–4, 1863, where famed Confederate general Thomas J. "Stonewall" Jackson received his mortal wound. Federal batteries with grape and canister had opened fired upon the enemy forces, which included members of the 23rd North Carolina Confederate Infantry, resulting in the killing or wounding of about twenty men. These individuals soon began "shrieking loudly for help."

Gen. Joseph Hooker asked for a detail of volunteers to leave Federal lines in an attempt to "bring in some of the enemy, that they might be cared for." Thomas Thompson, Henry Heller, Wallace W. Cranston, and Elisha B. Seaman came forward, assisted by a John B. Runyon. Seaman recalled,

We climbed over our works and advanced to where the wounded men lay, but succeeded only in bringing one man back, whom we carried to the Chancellorsville House. During all this time we were under a heavy skirmish fire.

Henry Heller provided more details of the event:

It was on the second day of the fight at Chancellorsville that General Hooker called for five men of my company to volunteer to enter the enemy's lines under a heavy fire from both sides, and bring in a Confederate, who was in great distress through having his leg shot off by a ball from our battery, and I was one who went.[12]

Records of the 23rd North Carolina Infantry reveal the names of two individuals who lost a leg and were captured at the battle of Chancellorsville, both members of Co. E, James A. Suit and Samuel Clark. Private Clark is specifically stated to have been wounded and captured on the second day of the battle, May 3, 1863, and was later nominated for the "Badge of Distinction for gallantry at Chancellorsville."[13]

A member of the 2nd Vermont Regiment of Infantry, Pvt. Wilbur Fisk, recalled his experiences after the battle of Bank's Ford, Virginia, fought May 4, 1863. He and a Lt. Henry Haywood (or Hayward) strolled across the field, where they encountered "a good-looking rebel soldier."

We gave him a drink. "Will you do me a favor?" "Yes," says the Lieutenant. "I will do anything for you I can." "You are probably the last man I shall have a chance to speak to." He gave the Lieutenant his name and the name of his wife and her address. It was in Alabama. He gave his pocket book and some letters. I don't remember what they all were. He gave him a locket in which was the portrait of his wife and two children. He wanted the Lieutenant to write the circumstances of his death. We shook hands with him and left.

The line was moving to left—their right, and we would probably have to go into action again so we had no time to tarry. A few moments before that if I could have seen a shell fall into the rebel ranks and burst I would have swung my hat and shouted hurrah but I felt different then. . . . Those things were sent to a Vermont Member of Congress and the Lieutenant got word back that they would be forwarded to destination under flag of truce the first opportunity. By the way that was Senator [Justin Smith] Morrill.[14]

During the famous battle of Gettysburg, July 2, 1863, Col. M. J. Bulger of the 47th Alabama Infantry was wounded while attempting to "take and hold a crossroad in front of Little Round Top." Bulger after the war related how

a minie ball struck me just over the left nipple, passed through my body, and lodged under the right shoulder blade, where it still remains.

When I was wounded I nerved myself up to keep from falling, and eased myself down against a tree that grew out of a crevice of the rocks in such a way as to afford me a convenient and comfortable seat. When the men came to where I was they rallied and had a desparate fight, but were finally driven back.

While this was going on I was suffering intensely, and thought I should strangle with blood. I saw a Federal soldier coming in a direction that would bring him close to me, and determined to ask him for water when he came near enough. I said to him: "My good fellow, will you give me a drink of water? I am wounded and choking to death with blood."

Without halting he threw his hand to the back of his neck, caught the strap of his canteen and laid it down in my lap saying: "I have no water but there is whisky, a great deal better for you; drink it." He passed on a few steps, got down behind a rock, and commenced shooting my retiring men.[15]

Captured by Wofford's Georgia Brigade on July 2, 1863, at Gettysburg near the peach orchard was William M. Boggs of Co. F, 114th Pennsylvania

Infantry. A wounded rebel yelled, "Yank, for God's sake help me out of this!" According to Boggs, while the Union batteries "were raking that territory,"

> I put my right arm under him . . . almost carried him for probably a mile (under that fire it seemed fully ten miles) to a field hospital in a stone farm-house, and there deposited him. Before leaving each had learned that the other was the son of a widowed mother; and as I was already a prisoner and he expected to be, we exchanged our mother's addresses. . . .
>
> According to agreement, he wrote my mother, from Fort Delaware, and she promptly proceeded there, taking with her those tasty delicacies a dear, good mother knows how to furnish, and nursed him into convalescence. My mother dying suddenly took away that means of learning his name. I only know that he was a Georgian.[16]

David Mouat, of Co. G, 29th Pennsylvania Infantry, recollected an experience taking place on October 29, 1863, not long after an engagement. He remembered the words of a fellow Federal soldier from the West, who mentioned how they had gone over a field of corn to look at dead Rebels where they encountered

> one poor fellow almost cut in half and who seemed to be dead. As we were short of rations and his haversack was filled with corn bread, Charley McCloskey who was along, started to help himself. The poor fellow opened his eyes, we gave him a drink and left him. We shortly returned and the Johnny was gone. . . .[17]

A Federal chaplain of the 77th New York Infantry, Norman Fox, Jr., was present at the battle of Spotsylvania, Virginia, on May 8, 1864. A Confederate soldier, Pvt. Thomas J. Roberts of Co. I, 12th Regiment of Georgia Infantry, was shot during the conflict by a minié ball in the groin, inflicting a fatal wound. The chaplain and others aided the young Rebel as kindly as possible, learning also that other members of his family had previously been killed during the war. Fox relates:

While we were talking he asked for a drink of water. I brought it, and as I raised him to a sitting posture, so that he could drink, he leaned his head forward upon my shoulder, and without a struggle was dead. . . . Often since that night I have thought of that Southern soldier lad who died actually in my arms, as if in a mother's embrace, and I pen this reminiscence that possibly it may make known to some surviving comrade or dear one that in his last hour what little could be done for him was tenderly performed.[18]

During the battle of Drury's Bluff, Virginia, fought on May 16, 1864, Sgt. Thomas E. Osgood, of Co. C, 12th Regiment of New Hampshire Volunteers, was wounded in his leg, and soon found himself lying in an ambulance next to a Confederate soldier who was suffering severely from a bad wound in his thigh. Sergeant Osgood, noticing the perspiration in his enemy's face, raised himself up on his elbow and with his own handkerchief kindly wiped off the face and brow of the Confederate. After Osgood repeated this hospitable gesture, the Rebel finally exclaimed:

"Well, this is unexpectedly good and kind in you, Sergeant, but how strange! Here are two deadly enemies, side by side, and one is wiping the sweat from the other's brow."

"Enemies! I did not know that we were enemies before."

"Why, you belong to the Union Army, don't you?"

"Yes, I do."

"Well, I belong to what you call the rebel army."

"I am aware of that, but I see no reason why we should be enemies. I don't know as you ever injured me, or that I ever injured you, and why should we have any ill will toward each other?"

"What are you fighting us for then?"

"We are not fighting you. We are fighting what you call the Southern Confederacy, only wishing to injure you, as we are obliged to in order to destroy that; so we can have but one government. . . ."

"Well, I never looked at it in just that light before, but I reckon you are right about us fighters, if not on what we are fighting for."

"Yes, . . . and I trust you may yet live to enjoy the privileges and blessings of the very government that you and your comrades are now trying to destroy. What may I call your name?"

"My name is Madison A. Brown; I belong to the Twenty-fifth South Carolina regiment."[19]

Sergeant Osgood in years to come would reminiscence about the incident, but did not know that Madison A. Brown had died at Drury's Bluff that fateful day—but not before his "enemy" had performed an act of sympathy and compassion on his fallen foe.[20]

Also at the battle of Drury's Bluff, another incident of humanitarian aid was being acted out by members of the 124th Regiment of New York Volunteers. As the Union soldiers charged the Confederate works, Rebel colonel Daniel Shipman Troy of the 59th Alabama Infantry attempted to rally his men, but he was shot through the lung by Federal private George W. Tompkins and was left on the field for dead. Capt. Thomas Taft, of Co. C, described the event as follows:

> The Colonel was shot through the breast. We carried back a great many wounded. . . . After it was all over and my men had given vent to their feelings in three rousing cheers, I dispatched a guard to the rear with the prisoners and a messenger for Surgeon Montfort; after which we with the utmost care and tenderness gathered up the wounded and conveyed them to the only building left standing in our immediate rear, and gave them water, and staunched the best we could the flow of blood from their wounds, my men in several instances holding their thumbs pressed against the severed arteries of their late foes until Surgeon Montfort with his assistants arrived and relieved them.
>
> Colonel Troy had been shot through the lungs and was suffering intense bodily pain. . . . He spoke with difficulty, but when I approached him as he lay upon the floor in

the house, to arrange a blanket which one of my men had folded as a pillow for him, but which was slipping from under his head, he . . . thank[ed] me for the unexpected kindness which had been showered upon him.[21]

One of the most touching accounts of the war, as well as the lack of animosity felt between members of the opposing army long after the conflict, is demonstrated in the writings of successful Philadelphia architect Frank H. Furness, who served as captain of Co. F, 6th Pennsylvania Cavalry. While at the battle of Cold Harbor, Virginia, on June 1, 1864, Captain Furness assisted a wounded Confederate soldier. He recalled the following, as printed in papers throughout the Southern states:

> The open space from the point where the Rebels turned and retreated to the belt of woods was strewn with their dead, dying and wounded, and thirty yards in front of the breastwork lay a wounded soldier, who made frantic and terrible attempts to regain his footing, but he was sorely wounded, and, after a few struggles, stretched himself exhausted on his back.
>
> An officer of the Union forces [Furness], seeing the sad plight of his wounded adversary, took a canteen of water from one of his sergeants, and, slinging it over his shoulder, jumped over the breastwork and ran to the wounded Confederate. When he arrived beside him, he found that he had been wounded in the lower part of the thigh, and his pantaloons from his knee to his foot were clotted with blood so that his leg looked like a dark red alligator hide.
>
> The officer asked the wounded man if he had a handkerchief. The Confederate replied that he had and that it was in the breastpocket of his jacket. . . . Binding the handkerchief tightly above the wound, he tried to make a tourniquet with his revolver. This, however, he could not do, the handerchief not being long enough, so he then passed it round the leg, crossing the ends, and, pulling them tight with all his strength, he knotted them above the wound, the knot pressing well into the leg, thus greatly staunching the flow of blood.

The officer then shifted the wounded man into as comfortable position as the ground would permit and scraped up with his hands the sandy soil to form a pillow for the head of the wounded man. "Now," said the officer, "this is all I can do for you, my man. I wish I could do more, but time flies and so must I. Here is a canteen of water. I'll leave it by your side. Good-bye."

The wounded man replied: "You may be a Yankee, but, by Gad, you are a gentleman."

And they parted; the officer went walking to the breastwork, and the poor, wounded Confederate—where? Did he die on the field, or was he found and cared for by his comrades, only to die of his wounds, or did he recover and live? What was the sequel? Who can tell? The officer got through the terrible war unhurt and is alive and well; but he would dearly like to know what became of the gallant soldier he left in such a plight.

There was one curious thing in connection with this incident that occurred to the officer in thinking the occurrence over, and that was that from the time of his kneeling beside the wounded man until he returned to the breastwork he was conscious of the fact that not one single shot from the Confederate line was fired at him. Shortly after the officer's return to the breastwork the rebels again advanced on it. . . .

Should this meet the eye of a Southern survivor of that horrible day, who can in any way recall or is cognizant of such an incident as has been above described, if he will kindly communicate with Captain Frank Furness he will in a measure gratify the desire on the part of the officer to know the end of it all. But there is only one chance in ten thousand that a sequel to this unfinished story will come to light.

Within some two weeks from the time Captain Furness published the above account throughout the South in various newspapers, he received a reply from Macon, Georgia, dated August 20, 1905, from a Mr. Green

W. Hodge, who had served as a private in Co. A, of the 9th Florida Infantry. He wrote:

> My Dear Friend and Kind Preserver. It is with feelings of the greatest gratitude that I write this. I saw your card in the paper entitled "Trying to find an old foe."
>
> There is no one knows what passed through my mind at the time you so bravely came to my relief; I thought then that I was a goner, and while lying there on the bare ground with what you scraped together for my headrest, I prayed that you might be spared for your noble act, and many times since that in my devotions to Almighty God, I have prayed that you might yet live and that some day I could see and thank you in person for your noble act, for I shall always believe that you saved my life on that occasion. . . .
>
> I was carried to the hospital and after several months recovered and was ordered back to the trenches and was again wounded at Petersburg, Va., on the day of the blowup, by the middle finger of my right hand being cut off with a piece of shell.
>
> I was a private in Finigan's Brigade of Florida Troup. After the war I went back to Florida and educated myself the best I could, and finally got to be high sheriff of my County, served four years, after which I married and went to farming and raised a family of four children. . . . When the Spanish-American War was declared I gave money to make up a company and went myself as a volunteer, a private, and helped free Cuba. But let me assure you that during all those forty years I have never failed to send up a silent prayer for the safety and well being of my unknown kind preserver. I thank God this day that my prayer has been heard and answered. I am now almost sixty-six years old and I feel that I can't last much longer; and now, kind friend, should we never be permitted to meet on this earth, may it please The Good Master above that when we come to die we may meet beyond this vale

where war is unknown, where nothing but happiness awaits those who have acted it so nobly here.

Now I wish that I could take you by the hand that so kindly bound up my wound and gave me the canteen of water, and thank you before I die for what you did for me on that bloody battlefield.

Almost half of my company was either killed or wounded in that fight. My old wounded thigh often troubles me as I grow older. If you remember, it is my left thigh. . . . If you will write me, in my next letter, I will send you my picture. . . . I hope you can read this but I doubt it. My hands are so cramped from old age and hardships that I can hardly write at all.

As can be imagined, Capt. Frank Furness was elated to receive the above reply, and wrote once again to Green W. Hodge from Philadelphia, on August 23, 1905. A portion of his letter to Mr. Hodge read:

Your letter of August 20th was handed to me this morning by Mr. Charles F. Grant, who, by the way, is an Ex-Confederate, having served with Col. Moseby in the first part and in the Confederate Navy in the latter part of the War, and it was through him, and with his consent, that I made the inquiry in regard to finding my old foe.

Words are wanting and I can in no way tell you how deeply I was affected by your letter when I found that the, to me, almost hopeless task of identifying my brave and gallant adversary was accomplished. . . .

We must contrive to personally meet that I may have the honor of grasping not one, but both hands of the gallant fellow whose sufferings I was fortunate enough to have the opportunity of alleviating, in a slight degree, as he lay wounded and, as I then thought, dying on the blood-stained ground of that fierce and frightful battlefield of Cold Harbor. . . .

Is it not strange that although at that time we were most bitter enemies, we have drunk from the same canteen and by so doing created the strongest possible bond of friendship between us?![22]

After the Civil War, E. B. Surface, the son of Jacob Surface who had served in Co. F, of the 36th Virginia Infantry, published a query in the *Confederate Veteran*, unsuccessfully requesting information relative to an incident occurring at the battle of Piedmont, June 5, 1864, in the Valley of Virginia. His father, having been wounded in the fray, was assisted by a Federal soldier, "a little man [who] kindly took up my bleeding father, assisted him to a spring, performed some additional act of kindness, told him good-by, and hastened on."[23]

On the battlefield near Lynchburg, Virginia, on June 17, 1864, Capt. Cread Milstead of Co. E, 5th West Virginia Volunteer Infantry, found Capt. R. H. Phelps, Virginia Cavalry, originally from La Grange, Texas, who lost his right leg as a result of his wounds. Phelps was taken by Milstead and Chaplain Joseph Little to the Federal headquarters and soon delivered "into the hands of the hospital attendants." Milstead wrote:

> Every 17th of June, from 1864 to 1891, I have never failed to think of this incident, and would wonder whether my friend Phelps had survived his wounds and was still living.
>
> On June 30, 1891, I sent a detailed account of the incident to the Wheeling, West Va., Register, which was published, and Sergeant Joseph C. Mcohen, one of Capt. Phelps' comrades, seeing it, wrote me at once, giving me his post-office address. . . . We have been corresponding with each other regularly ever since 1891, have exchanged photographs of ourselves and families, and our correspondence will be continued as long as we both live. . . .
>
> I have yet to meet one who bears any animosity or ill feeling towards the true soldiers of the Southern Army.[24]

George H. Blakeslee of Co. G, 129th Illinois Infantry, issued a similar query as he recalled an incident of the Peach Tree Creek battle in Georgia, of July 20, 1864:

> There was opposed to us that day Featherstone's brigade of Mississippians, composed of the First Mississippi Sharp-

shooters, Twenty-Second, Thirty-First, Thirty-Third, and Fortieth Mississippi Regiments. When the charging line of Stewart's braves came surging on against a line of veteran bluecoats . . . there fell, within twenty paces of our regimental line, a mere boy, having both feet carried away by a shell.

As soon as the fiercest of the attacks were past, humanity brought him assistance, although we were even yet under fire. We ligatured his limbs to stop the bleeding, which was rapidly sapping his young life. If he still lives, this writer would like to know if he remembers a Federal captain who picked him up and carried him away from the battle and back to the Federal field hospital.[25]

From the "Officers' Hospital" at Annapolis, Maryland, in June of 1864, a Federal soldier remembered events during the "second day in the Wilderness," in the month of May. As he reclined at the foot of a tree, wrapped in his overcoat, he noticed that

a few yards from me lay the Adjutant of the 9th Ala., seriously, and probably mortally wounded. His cries of anguish were truly heart rending. He was a rebel, but human; and our compassionate surgeon administered to him the few grains of morphine which he had reserved for our own suffering braves.

He believed that the hour of his departure was close at hand. . . . It was about midnight when, attracted by his cries . . . , a few rough, warm hearted Northmen gathered around him. He said that he had once been a Christian, but he had wandered in forbidden paths. He besought some one to pray with him. Our warm and gentle hearted Surgeon knelt by his side, and others bent reverentially around, and there in the solemn hush of midnight, there in the very presence of our foes, the earnest, tender, pleading voice of prayer went up to the great All-Father in behalf of him our enemy, now enemy no longer.

Never did this unnatural slaughter seem so horrible, never did this cursed Rebellion seem so groundless and so devilish, as by the revelation of that midnight prayer.[26]

In a letter to his wife dated August 22, 1864, and referenced as "Before Petersburg, Va.," Col. Byron M. Cutcheon of the 20th Michigan Infantry remarked that during the siege he was in the act of taking a Rebel lieutenant prisoner. At first the Confederate declined. As Cutcheon raised his sword, however, the man obeyed,

> but just as he sprang over the pit, he was hit by a bullet from his own friends, who intended it for me. He fell just by me, his head in the abattis. He begged pitifully to be carried to the rear; but I told him I could not get my own men carried to the rear then. I gave him some drink and a lemon, and spread a rubber blanket over him to keep the sun off, and there I left him. I could do no more. I did not learn his name or regiment.[27]

Writing home to his mother from the "Dismal Swamp, or Yellow House," on August 23, 1864, Pvt. John L. Smith, of Co. K, 118th Pennsylvania Infantry, related that

> in this fight we captured six battle flags . . . and took a great many prisoners. The corn field on our right was full of killed and wounded Rebels and I went out a few moments after the fight and had a talk with many of the wounded Rebels. Some of them took it cool and others were groaning and crying. I cut a canteen off a dead Rebel. It was full of water. I gave it to another wounded Rebel and then I picked up a canteen of water and gave it to another one. I told them to cheer up and they would soon be carried off the field to our hospital. They were South Carolina troops from Beauregard's army.[28]

A former member of Co. I, 11th Pennsylvania Infantry Cavalry or 108th Regiment, John R. Brink, related after the war an incident that took place on October 7, 1864, at Darbytown, near Richmond, Virginia. Sgt. James G. Keech of Co. B, the color-bearer for the regiment, encountered Rebel colonel Alexander C. Haskell of the 7th South Carolina Cavalry. A skirmish ensued, leaving Colonel Haskell "with a bullet in him" as he fell from his horse. Brink re-creates the story:

When the colonel fell Sergt. Keech saw that he had a very nice pair of spurs on. He jumped off to get them, when he saw a large and beautiful gold ring on the colonel's finger. He thought he was dead, and was about to take the ring off his finger, when the colonel spoke and said: "Take anything, but leave me this ring."

The sergeant then told him if he lay there somebody would take it, and if the opportunity ever offered that he would give or send him the ring. He then took the ring and spurs, and the papers out of his pocket, in the presence of several rebels who were sitting on their horses nearby.

Some twelve years later, in 1876, Keech observed Haskell's name in the newspapers, and soon placed an ad in a number of Charleston, South Carolina, papers. Not long afterward, he received a reply from Haskell. Keech, through a friend of the former Confederate cavalry officer, kept his word, telling the colonel "that he still had in his possession the gold ring, and was ready, and in fact very anxious, to return it to him." Haskell replied, thanking him for his generosity, and the ring was returned.[29]

A native of Clinton County, Pennsylvania, Thomas F. Dornblazer, who became a Lutheran minister in Lee County, Illinois, after the Civil War, served in the 7th Pennsylvania Cavalry during the conflict. Writing in 1884, he related an event of October 13, 1864, at the battle of Rome, Georgia. He wrote in his diary account:

After firing a few shots, I saw a rebel officer leaping the fence twenty yards to my right, and starting to run across the open field to join his comrades. In his right hand he held a navy revolver, and in his left an officer's sword. I leveled my "Spencer" and ordered him, sharply, to halt and throw down his arms, which he did. But seeing that I was altogether alone, he seized his weapons again, sprang to the stump of a broken tree . . . fired two shots from his revolver, and said in a defiant tone, "I'll fight you!" . . .

I took my horse by the rein, and made a left about wheel, two paces to the rear, taking position on the left side of my horse. My antagonist in the meantime fired two more shots, wounding my horse in the hip; and mistaking my maneuvers for a retreat, he rushed forward and preemptorily demanded my surrender. He came to the fence . . . [and] was in the act of stepping across when I ordered him a second time to halt. My gun was leveled; he raised his revolver with a threat: I fired! His arm dropped without discharging his revolver. His tall form sank to the ground as he exclaimed, "I'm a dead man."

At once I dropped my carbine, and offered him my hand; he gave it a friendly grasp and said, "You have killed a good man." "I'm sorry for it," said I, "and why did you take up your arms again?" Said he, "I made a vow that I would never surrender to one man. You were the only man I saw, and I determined to fight you, and get possession of your horse—then I could have made my escape. You did your duty, but you might have surrendered to me."

After making him as comfortable as I could with overcoat and blanket, I inquired his name and rank. He said his name was William H. Lawrence, Captain and acting Colonel of the Eighth Alabama cavalry. He said he had a wife and two dear children living at Tuscaloosa, Alabama. His wife and daughter were devoted Christians, and he lamented that he had not lived a better life in the army. He did not feel prepared to die. He knew that he must die.

The ball struck the corner of his belt-plate and passed through his body, inflicting a mortal wound. His mind was perfectly clear, and for one-half hour we were alone, undisturbed, and we wept and prayed together, invoking the Infinite Mercy of God to forgive us both. Seeing the bugler of our regiment at a distance, I called to him to bring up a stretcher to carry back a wounded officer.

We carried him three-quarters of a mile to the field hospital, and had his wounds dressed. Before I left him he gave me his diary, and requested me to send it to his wife, and tell her that he died happy. After his death next day, the surgeon found on his person a ten-dollar gold piece, and a signet-ring with his wife's photograph set in it, in miniature.

After the war, Dornblazer wrote to Captain Lawrence's widow, and informed her

> that he had in his possession a sword and revolver which belonged to her husband, who fell in battle near Rome, Georgia, and if she desired it, he would forward them to her by express. She said her husband wrote her on the morning of that fatal day, and feared the results of the approaching conflict.
>
> She said her boy "Willie," eleven years old, would like to have his papa's sword. The sword and revolver were forwarded immediately, and a prompt answer came back, with many thanks from the mother and her son.[30]

The assistant quartermaster and lieutenant of the 9th Tennessee Federal Cavalry, E. H. Matthews, participated in the battle of Morristown, Tennessee, October 28, 1864. The short battle against fellow Tennesseans in the Confederate forces ended in the evening, with the sounds of "groans and pleading for water." Matthews relates:

> I found two Federal soldiers standing over a wounded soldier cursing him and threatening to kill him, as they said he was a spy and had on a "Yankee overcoat." The man on the ground was a wounded Confederate soldier, and protested that he had picked up the overcoat in a skirmish and was no spy. . . .
>
> I ordered the two who were standing over the wounded man not to kill him, but to go back to their commands if they couldn't help take care of the wounded without butchering them. The wounded soldier was shivering from the cold, as his "Yankee overcoat" had been taken from him, and I took my blanket from under my saddle and wrapped it around the wounded man and asked him what was his name. He gave me the name of Gid T. Smith, of Gen. Vaughn's old regiment, the Third

Tennessee Confederate Infantry. He said he belonged to a company that was raised in Meigs County, Tenn., where I was born and raised.

Humanity demanded that I put this poor fellow where he could get the service of a surgeon and where he wouldn't freeze to death. . . . About this time I heard approach what I knew from the noise on the frozen ground (for it was night) was a body of cavalry. I knew that if I made myself known and they were Confederates I should probably be made a prisoner. I knew also that I couldn't move the man myself, and if he couldn't get relief at once he would die. I took the risk, hailed the approaching column, made myself known, and, as it turned out, the command was part of my own regiment, commanded by Capt. D. M. Nelson.

I made known the facts, Capt. Nelson made a detail and sent back to our camp for an ambulance, and we gathered together some wood, built a fire, and remained with this wounded "Johnny Reb" until the ambulance came and took the wounded man back to the hospital.

I ascertained that the wounded man had been shot through the lower part of the bowels, the ball passing through him, and that he was a son of Capt. Jack Smith, an old and honored citizen who resided near Decatur, in Meigs County, Tenn. I wrote to his father, whom I knew well, and he came to Knoxville and nursed his boy to health.

That wounded soldier is now the postmaster at Census Post Office, Meigs County, Tenn., and has been partly paralyzed from that wound since the night of October 28, 1864. He has a fine wife and family of children as can be found in the State of Tennessee.

I am an old man now, and write this simply as matters of that kind ought not to be lost. All of us know that "war is hell," but many such acts occurred which should not be lost to history."[31]

During the battle of Trevillian Station, Virginia, on June 11, 1864, Federal captain Noble D. Preston, of the 10th New York Cavalry, was wounded severely during a heroic charge that earned him a Medal of Honor. He was taken by litter off the battlefield to a log house filled with the dead and wounded from both the Federal and Confederate forces. Preston described the scene as a chamber of horrors, as he listened to "the awful moanings and piteous cries of the suffering and dying."

Remembering that fateful day, Preston later recalled:

> It was late in the evening, when a fine appearing young Confederate Officer was brought in and placed on the old straw mattress by my side. He was very pale and weak, and was evidently suffering much pain. To my inquiry as to the nature of his injuries he said that his spine was fractured. A bullet had entered his right hip, the wound being similar to my own, except that in my case, the bullet had passed the spine without injury to it.
>
> I learned from him that his name was Russell, a Major of the 7th Georgia Cavalry. He mentioned the disastrous result of the day's fighting to his regiment, and as his voice grew weaker, his thoughts wandered to the far away home and the loved ones, whom he mentioned with emotion.[32]

After the Civil War, Captain Preston published an account of the battle of Trevillian Station and his experiences in the August 28, 1880, issue of the *Philadelphia Times.* He related that Russell

> was conscious that his life was of short duration, and expressed a desire to see the colonel of his regiment, who was a prisoner in our hands. His request was granted and the colonel under a guard, was sent to him. . . . In the brief interval that I was permitted to know Major Russell he presented the evidences of a noble character. He was youthful, and although his eyes were sunken and his countenance pallid, he was a fine-looking fellow. . . .
>
> It was near midnight when the spirit of Major Russell took its flight, and with the lifeless form by my side, I was left to contemplate the horrors of war. . . . As I lay on the litter of straw with the dead Confederate major, a flickering light from a burning faggot in the fire-place cast a

sickening light over the wretched room, in which, scattered around on the floor, lay about a dozen wounded and dead soldiers, the blue and gray lying side by side.

In a few days after publishing his account in the *Philadelphia Times,* Captain Preston received a letter from Oaklawn, Lookout Mountain in Tennessee. The correspondence hailed from Anna Russell Cole, who wrote:

> The Major Russell who died by your side "on a straw mattress in an old log-house" was my brother, Major Whiteford Doughty Russell, oldest son of Hon. H. F. Russell, of Augusta, Ga. He was wounded on the 11th of June, 1864, and died on the 14th. . . . He had been married five years, and was the father of two children, girls. He had returned from a visit to his family but a day or two before he was killed. . . .
>
> More than sixteen years have gone slowly and wearily by to us since the day you were carried into that log-hut and laid by the side of the dying man who had filled so many lives with happiness. . . . Today your hand has lifted the tear-besprinkled veil which separated us from the terrible hour when the news of his death came.
>
> We have often longed for more definite information of his last hours than we have heretofore been able to obtain; and are grateful that an appreciative soul was near him in that final struggle.[33]

Maj. Whiteford D. Russell had originally served as a member of the "Walker Light Infantry," of Richmond County, Georgia, which entered the Confederate service as Co. I, 1st Georgia Infantry.[34] Such amiable and endearing correspondence as the above, between residents of the North and South, did much to quickly heal the wounds of the two regions and facilitate the reunification of the United States after the war, in both mind and spirit, as well as by geography.

Maryland Confederate guerilla leader Col. Harry Gilmor recalled at war's end an incident with the "Jessie Scouts," or soldiers organized by Union general John C. Frémont who dressed in Confederate uniforms and served as spies. On one occasion he and a Federal scout were riding together, the latter on a mission to capture a Rebel at a local resident's home. Gilmor related:

> There was a gate leading into a lane near where we stood. It was a little way open, and he made a desperate effort to get through; but his horse pushed it to with his neck, and at the same instant my sword went through his body. He fell off, dead in less than five minutes, but not before he said, "You sold me pretty well, but I don't blame you."
>
> I gave him whisky and water out of my flask, and tried to save him, but my blade went too near the heart. He had a very good saddle, that suited me better than my own; the handcuffs I carried all the way to Gettysburg, and there gave them away.[35]

In an issue of *Crutch,* a Civil War publication of the U.S.A. General Hospital at Annapolis, Maryland, an anonymous article by a Federal soldier pathetically revealed both the horror of the "fraternal war" as well as the humanity of the enemy toward one another, even in death. In the year 1864, near the city of Franklin, Tennessee, the Union soldier encountered "for the first time a rebel corpse," evidently a casualty of the battle of Franklin, fought on November 30.

> He lay with his head to the wall, stiff and stark, his feet stretched out towards the road. A bullet had entered under his right ear and came out beneath the left, where some of his brains could be seen hanging down. The stones around his head were besmeared with blood. His last ration lay beside him—a chunk of yellow corn cake and a very fat piece of raw pork.
>
> A man of twenty-five, clad in the coarse gray rebel suit, his left arm lying on the ground along his side, his right arm resting on his left breast, with light brown hair, and short cut reddish beard and moustache; his blue eyes, glassy and vacant, stared at the skies, with a ghastly gaze. Thus he had lain for a whole day and night, no one pitying, no one burying him: no friend to close his eyes. But he had been touched by some unhallowed hand, for his

pockets were turned inside out. I hoped that this deed was done by no soldier of ours; but I feared that it was before I left the spot.

I had been on a battle-field before, and I had looked on thousands of wounded men before but it happened that this was the first rebel corpse I had seen. I got off my horse and stood near the dead man. . . .

I was greatly moved with pity for the rebel; and turning to a soldier on horseback beside me, I said that I thought some one ought to close the dead man's eyes.

"Oh he's well enough," was the gruff response. . . .

He looked away. I saw that I might now do safely, and without arousing any suspicion of my own loyalty, what my heart urged me do for the poor rebel, I knelt down and shut his eyes, and then rode off.

And as I thought that if the war went on, perhaps a Northern boy I knew might yet lie, stark and stiff, as this man now lay, on some Southern highway, with no one to pity him or to close his eyes, and that, in some far away log hut, a young widow or a loving mother might soon have to weep for this new made corpse hat my hand had touched.

I saw almost as little for some minutes as the glassy eyes of the rebel soldier had seen since the bullet gave him his last long furlough.[36]

CHAPTER 5

Civilians and Soldiers

MANY YEARS AGO, A FRIEND BORN AND RAISED IN GEORGIA REMARKED how she was practically a teenager before she realized that the derogatory term "damn-Yankee" was, in reality, "two words instead of one." This remark aptly summarizes the concept and stereotype that both scholars and lay persons have believed exemplified the feelings between invading troops or occupational forces of both armies and those of civilians. Bitterness, hostility, and animosity certainly existed, as revealed by contemporary accounts, yet compassion and humanitarian aid were also demonstrated in many instances.

An officer with the 81st Pennsylvania Regiment, Lt. James H. Walker, recorded in his diary entry for May 12, 1862, his visit to the village of "Burnt Ordinary" located in James City County, Virginia. A dwelling house, a store, barn, and some Negro shanties and outbuildings composed the settlement. Walker relates how "it had evidently been a flourishing place once—but had suffered from our stragglers more than a little."

> I entered into conversation with the lady of the house, a middle-aged, but rather good looking woman. . . . I found that her husband had fled at the approach of our troops, that her son was in the Secession Army and that marauding bands of our stragglers had carried off or destroyed everything of value which she possessed—

I immediately deposited the contents of my haversack in her lap and procured her a supply of coffee and hard bread from our wagon— This display of kindness melted her southern nature and her tears flowed freely as she declared how much she had been mistaken in the character of the northern people as a body.[1]

The wife of Minor Meriwether, an officer in the Confederate army, Mrs. Elizabeth Avery Meriwether, recalled after the war an experience with the occupational forces of the Federal army in the city of Memphis, Tennessee. Union forces had successfully seized the city in a naval battle on June 6, 1862, after which Gen. Ulysses S. Grant's troops came into the city and erected a "line of pickets," with one "picket post" of some fifteen or twenty men located directly in front of the Meriwether home.

Minor Meriwether had fought at the battle of Shiloh, and his black body servant had captured a Union sword that he brought home to his master's son as a souvenir. Mrs. Meriwether recalled:

One day a soldier from the Picket Post by our front gate came to our door and said to me:

"Your little boy has been playing out by the gate; I heard him say you have a Yankee sword and that you had hidden it on top of your book case. Now, I don't care a rap how many swords you have . . . but a lot of fellows might feel differently about it. If they heard of it they might make trouble for you."

"What must I do?" I asked.

"I will take it away for you, if you wish."

I pointed to the book case and told him to take the sword which Henry [her husband's body servant] had brought back from Shiloh; he did so, and no doubt this soldier's kindness saved me great trouble. I knew of instances where women were thrown in prison for having a weapon in their homes.

A few days after this sword incident I saw two soldiers leading our cow out of the back lot and it worried me greatly. Milk was the chief article of food of my two little boys. What could I give them in place of milk? . . . I took my two little boys by the hand . . . carrying a tin bucket

. . . and we marched down to the Picket Post by the gate. Around a smoldering fire were a dozen or so soldiers.

"Good evening, soldiers," I said politely. "I have come to ask you to be kind enough to give me some milk for my children's supper. Our cow is a fine milker. . . . A quart will do for my little ones."

For a moment there was dead silence; the men stared at me but spoke no word. I began to fear my boys would go to bed supperless. Then one of the soldiers broke into a good natured laugh.

"Of course the little Rebs shall have some milk for their supper," he said. "What do you say, Boys?"

"Sure, let 'em have some," cried a chorus of voices. "Gimme your bucket, Sonny," said the first speaker; little Avery stared at the big bearded soldier as he handed him the tin bucket. The soldier patted the child on the head. "I've got a little shaver at home," he said, "a boy just about this one's age. I guess his mother would feel bad if he couldn't get any milk for his supper. Just wait here, Marm. I'll be back in a minute."

We waited by the gate and very soon the soldier came back with the tin bucket full of milk.

"Thank you so much," I said gratefully. "May I have some every day?"

"Sure you may. Bring your bucket every morning and evening. I'll fill it for you."

From that time on the big bearded soldier kept us supplied with milk; true, it was the milk of my own cow, nevertheless I felt very grateful. Had those soldiers not been kind hearted they could have kept all the milk for themselves and my two little boys would have had nothing but very dry bread for their suppers.[2]

Sometime in July 1863, sixteen-year-old Cornelia Barrett was residing at "Newstead," the "Barrett Plantation" located near Jackson, Hinds County, Mississippi. Federal forces were active in the area and conflict with Confederate troops was inevitable. Eventually the Barrett home served as a hospital for the wounded and dying of both armies. Cornelia Barrett Ligon later recalled:

There were over a hundred wounded Confederates and a large number of Yankees. Among the mortally wounded was a very young Yankee. He was placed on our front gallery to die. As I passed by him, he beckoned me to come closer and I bent over him to hear what he said. He asked me to write a letter to his sweetheart to whom he was engaged to marry. I wrote just as he dictated, telling how he loved her and wanted her to remain true to him, and they would meet in the Great Beyond.

He asked me to send her a plain gold ring which he took from his finger and requested that I cut a lock of his hair and send that also. The scene was pathetic and tears rolled down my cheeks as I did what he requested. We made the boy as comfortable as possible, but he died that night.

I asked the young lady to please reply on receipt of my message so that I would be sure she received it, but it was six months before I heard from her. In her letter she expressed profound gratitude to me for what I had done.[3]

A quartermaster of Co. F, 16th Pennsylvania Cavalry from Columbia County, John Daniel Follmer, while in Virginia on April 30, 1863, recorded in his diary of a visit to the Kelly residence at "Kelly's Ford." He indignantly remarked:

Plundering does not seem to be right. The house was entered and ladies insulted. The men also broke into a sick lady's chamber, and insulted the husband in her presence. These men claim to come from an enlightened country, but are a disgrace to the army. If the man was guilty of wrong-doing he should be punished, but under no circumstances should a lady's sick chamber be invaded. This cannot help us conquer an enemy. The man who did the deed should be punished and made an example.[4]

On October 24, 1863, Lt. Col. James Cornell Biddle, 27th Pennsylvania Infantry, writing home to his wife in Philadelphia from the headquarters of the Army of the Potomac at Warrenton, Virginia, related his experience in dealing with friends of the family residing in the area:

We saw Mrs. Pollock and her daughter. . . . She asked
after Aunt and Uncle Latimer, and said the war had pro-
duced no effect upon her feelings for her old friends. . . .
She spoke of her troubles, and told us she had lost her
only son, who was on Gen. Kemper's Staff, and was killed
at Gettysburg. They have not got anything to live upon,
everything they had having been taken from them. . . .

I told them I would assist them as far as lay in my
power, but I believed they were required to take the oath
of allegiance before they could get anything from the
Commissary Department. It is a pretty hard case, and I
feel very sorry for them. Their condition is only a sample
of the others living in this neighborhood.

Later, on October 28 and 30, Biddle tells of the troubles and plight of
a "Mrs. Murray," whose lawn had become the headquarters of Gen. Alfred
Pleasonton. She complained to Biddle that

[s]he had heard a great deal said about the doings of
Union officers, but always disbelieved them—that she
had always been for the Union herself but that now she
felt herself inclined to go the other way. . . . I told Gen.
Meade what she had said, and he sent for Gen. Pleasan-
ton, and told him he did not wish him to remain there. I
asked if I could do anything and offered, this at Dr. Let-
terman's request, any assistance in the way of Medical advice or medicine.

When I first saw her I thought from her appearance
that she was about being confined, but she brought her
baby to show us, which she said was only two months old
(Charlie Cadwalader said he thought it must be a dropsi-
cal affection). She was very nervous and cried during the
interview.

It is very hard for those who are living in this neighborhood. She said they only had enough to live by from day
to day, and we are unable to assist them, as they are
obliged to take the oath of allegiance and then swear it is
absolutely necessary to prevent them from starving—and
then they can only get sufficient to last them for five days.[5]

Confederate general John B. Gordon recalled an incident of the war echoing the above account. Gen. Newton M. Curtis of New York was stationed in Virginia near Fairfax Courthouse, when a woman came into the Union lines to obtain food for her household. Gordon states:

> The orders required all applicants for supplies to take the oath of allegiance to the United States before such supplies could be furnished. This hungry and wan woman was informed that she could have the necessaries for which she asked upon subscribing to that oath. What was she to do? Her kindred, her husband and son, were soldiers in the Confederate army. If she refused to take the oath, what would become of her and those dependent upon her? If she took the oath, what was to become of her own convictions and her loyalty to the cause of those she loved? It is not necessary to say that her sense of duty and her fidelity to the Southern cause triumphed. Sad and hungry, she turned away, resolved to suffer on. But General Curtis was in that camp. . . .
>
> He had . . . in his private purse some of the money which he had earned as a soldier, and he illustrated in his character that native knighthood which ennobles its possessor while protecting, befriending, and blessing the weak or unfortunate. It is enough to add that this brave and suffering Virginia woman did not leave the Union camp empty-handed.[6]

A Civil War museum in Gettysburg, Pennsylvania, at one time possessed a prayer book, since stolen, of a Rebel officer from Emanuel County, Georgia, who died on July 1, 1863 during that famous battle. Entering the service as a captain of Artillery in the Wright Legion, he fell at Gettysburg from a minié ball that "struck him just above the right temple, passing through the brain. He survived about 3 hours." His last words are said to have been that of "Mother, Mother." Though he was far away from his Georgia home, tradition has it that during his last hours, a local Gettysburg woman gave him water on the battlefield.[7]

Acts of humanitarianism and kindness during the Civil War often had profound and long-lasting effects that transcended and outlasted the war itself, as witnessed by the following account. In 1864 near Nashville,

Tennessee, Col. Thomas Jefferson Downey, commanding officer of the 15th Regiment of U.S. Colored Infantry, was stationed to guard the Nashville-Chattanooga railroad. At one point the regiment was encamped near the residence of wealthy landowner, slaveholder, and lawyer, Thomas Washington, who lived in the 5th Ward of the city of Nashville. The 15th Regiment, composed of free blacks and former slaves, soon became rebellious, attempted to seize Colonel Washington,

> threatened him with death, and also set about destroying the elegant family mansion. Col. Downey, by great exertions, and at the imminent risk of his own life, succeeded in rescuing Col. Washington from death, and saving the mansion and other property from destruction. Col. Washington felt profoundly grateful at the time for Col. Downey's brave exertions in his behalf, and promised never to forget them.

Colonel Downey left military service in December 1864 and returned home to Tiffin, the county seat of Seneca County, Ohio, though he had enlisted originally in the 113th Ohio Volunteer Infantry while a resident of Pickaway County.

By 1872 Downey had died, leaving his wife and family in destitute circumstances. Mrs. Downey was forced to "rely on her needle for support." A contemporary newspaper account, however, related that

> [s]he and their children lived in their humble way, with little thought that a great change was soon to be wrought in their condition. . . . Col. Washington died, when it was found that he had willed his property, consisting of ten thousand dollars in bonds and greenbacks and three hundred acres of improved land situated a mile and a half from Nashville—The whole valued at a hundred thousand dollars at least—to the heirs of Col. Downey.[8]

The former Federal officer's son, Israel J. Downey, went to Nashville and discovered everything in the will as stated. The administrator of Colonel Washington's estate went to Tiffin, Ohio, to arrange details of the transfer of property. Thus an act of kindness of an enemy toward his foe rescued a family from poverty and earned it a fortune.

A noncommissioned officer in the 97th Pennsylvania Infantry, Cpl. Thomas Clark, writing home to his sister on April 3, 1864 from Fernandine, Florida, mentioned:

> There was eight of us went out in a sail boat 30 miles away from camp, after a rebel deserter's wife and two children, and they were hard looking cases, for they had no more clothes than covered their nakedness and pretty nearly starved into the bargain, when we give them some of our bread they were as much pleased with it as I would be with a mince pie. They said they had not eat any bread for over two years and coffee. The same what they make coffee out of is burnt corn.[9]

The stories of the depredations, atrocities, and destructions of Gen. William Tecumseh Sherman's troops in their famous "march to the sea" in 1864 are well-known. Little is known, however, of the Union general's permission to have "Santa Claus" visit the children of Savannah in December of that year.

During the Christmas season of 1864, Union soldiers of Sherman's forces were far away from hearth and home, and many of them were fathers of young children. Spencer B. King, in one of his famed "Civil War Centennial Columns," which appeared for a number of years in the *Macon [Georgia] Telegraph-News,* relates the details:

> One company of occupying troops talked it over and decided that to the best of their ability they would bring some joy to the Savannah children. [T]hey went to work improvising dolls from rags, making crude toys . . . taking food from their own rations. . . . All this they gathered up and placed on a wagon, which they decorated in gay colors, making it look as much like Santa's sleigh as possible. The mules that pulled the wagon were even fitted with improvised antlers to resemble, not too closely, reindeer.
>
> They picked by lot a sergeant of the company to dress as Santa Claus and drive the wagon about the town delivering the presents and food to the homes in the city.[10]

In the winter of 1865, while Sherman's troops were burning Columbia, South Carolina, Federal lieutenant John A. McQueen, of the 15th Illinois Cavalry, assisted the family of Dr. William Reynolds from having its home destroyed during the wanton conflagration. Some "forty homeless ones found shelter there" during the weeks and months that followed. McQueen recorded the following in his diary: "It was heartrending to see the destruction of property, and the insults visited upon the defenseless women and children by our Union soldiers. I did all I could to prevent it but was powerless."

A postwar newspaper account related:

> When about to leave with the army, Dr. R. handed him [McQueen] a letter of thanks, signed by two Episcopal clergymen, whose families were refugees in the house and himself. The facts were stated and he was kindly commended to Confederate troops, should the fortune of war cause him to be taken prisoner.
>
> Dr. R. said to him, that as the army was going to Camden, and that town would probably be also burned, he begged that Lieut. McQueen would take care of the poor old blind Bishop Davis, which he promised to do. Upon his arrival there he procured a guard and placed it around the Bishop's premises and protected them during the conflagration, so that no Federal soldiers entered the gate.

A day or two after the above-noted event at Camden, Lt. John McQueen was involved in a skirmish on Lynch's Creek at Mount Elon, South Carolina, near Tiller's Bridge, on February 28, 1865. While commanding a group of scouts, McQueen was "shot through the abdomen." The officer

> was severely wounded and when about to be bayoneted by soldiers, infuriated at Sherman's destruction of Columbia and Camden, showed the letter he had in his pocket; it saved his life. He was taken to a farmhouse, and notice was sent to Camden. A friend of Bishop Davis procured a vehicle and rode fifteen miles to where he was; carried to Camden, he received the kindest attention.

One of the clergymen alluded to, the Reverend Toomer
Porter, heard of Lieutenant McQueen's sad misfortune,
and though one hundred miles off, went to Camden and
remained with him until he could travel. He then obtained a carriage and carried him to Hillsboro, to General
Johnston, procured a parole, and sent him home.

There were many such incidents in the war . . . and no
doubt on both sides.[11]

Oral tradition preserves a touching account of a civilian aiding a soldier. The soldier was Albert Tinsley Glazner, originally from Transylvania
County, North Carolina. Sometime in 1863, Glazner was "workin' out in
the cornfield and was taken from the field"—that is, forcibly conscripted
into the Confederate army. Official records show his enlistment on December 20, 1863, in Orange County, Virginia, into Co. B, 6th Regiment
of North Carolina State Troops. Sources also reveal how Glazner deserted
on February 7, 1864. According to family legend, "the first battle he went
into he deserted and joined the Union Army." He frequently related to his
grandchildren that, after the war,

[h]e was up in Virginia, walking along Iron Bridge Road,
in Chesterfield County, and became ill and collapsed. He
hid or crawled underneath the bridge, where he became
unconscious. [W]hen he came to, there was an old black
man feeding him. He said, "You've been very sick and I've
been feedin' and lookin' after you. I'm going to get you
back to your side, because you're fightin' for my freedom."

The slave was sneakin' out at night to help him. The
old colored man, during the night, once he was better,
carried him across the river on his shoulders, and said,
"Your men are right up there."[12]

As can be seen in the accounts detailed above, acts of kindness between
soldiers and civilians, as well as among the fighting men in the field, occurred in a variety of situations. Similar examples of hospitality during the
Civil War can be found within military prisons, North and South, and between guards and prisoners, as witnessed by the stories that unfold in the
following chapter.

CHAPTER 6

Prisons and Prisoners

THE NAMES OF CIVIL WAR MILITARY PRISONS, SUCH AS ELMIRA, ANDER-sonville, Belle Isle, Libby, Johnson's Island, and a host of others, conjure to the mind tales of atrocities, brutality, starvation, and rampant disease. Many accounts exist, however, that defy the stereotypical image of life as a prisoner of war. Not all captors were the epitome of evil and degradation—those who delighted in the suffering and humiliation of their captives. Nu-merous postwar writings by former prisoners successfully illustrate the horrors of incarceration, yet contemporary accounts equally demonstrate the attempt by many to soften, whenever possible, the deprivations and in-timidations of POW life. This humanity was extended, not only to the prisoners, but to their families as well.

During the winter of 1861–62, Col. James Edward Rains, of the 11th Tennessee Infantry, C.S.A., commanded the garrison at Cumberland Gap, Kentucky. Twenty-nine years of age in 1861 and a lawyer in civilian life, Rains had risen swiftly from the rank of private to colonel. Writing home to his young wife Ida on December 6, 1861, he related to her a heartrend-ing incident that had transpired only recently. He stated:

> I was riding out beyond the Gap a mile or two, when I
> met a couple of ladies on horse back, approaching the
> Gap. They were from London [Kentucky] and meeting

Col. James Edward Rains, 11th Tennessee Infantry (C.S.A.). COURTESY OF THE HISTORICAL SOCIETY OF PENNSYLVANIA, PHILADELPHIA.

me in the road, at once they recognized me, having seen me as I passed through that place. They told me that the husband and three sons of one, and two brothers of the other were prisoners of war at the Gap, having been taken at the Wildcat fight, and they had come to bring them some clean clothes and to try to see them, and they desired to know if I would pass them through the Gap.

Asking their names I found that it was Mrs. Jackson and Miss Pitman. I told Mrs. Jackson that her husband and three sons had been sent to Knoxville and she could not see them. She burst into tears. I then told Miss Pitman that one of her brothers had died, and the other was sick in the Hospital, but that it was entirely against the rules for her to go over to see him.

She commenced screaming and begging to be allowed to go over and see her sick brother and to get the remains of her dead brother. I readily agreed for her to have the remains, but told her firmly that I could not allow her to pass the Gap. I rode down a mile or two and when I returned she was still where I had left her at the foot of the mountain and both of them almost broken hearted.

They begged most piteously to be allowed to see the brother, said they would never go away until they had seen him, that I could not be so cruel and hard-hearted as to refuse them the privilege, that I had made [a] great character through their country among the women, by my kindness in protecting them, etc., etc., and that now I could not be so unkind as to refuse them the favor they asked, that they were willing to be taken through the works blind-folded.

Do you think I gave way and allowed them to pass? I am ashamed to acknowledge that I did. I could not help it. Their brother was disinterred today and they return with him tomorrow, leaving the sick brother in the Hospital.

How sad is war! These poor women come sixty or seventy miles to see their dearest friends on earth, one to see a husband and three sons, the other to see her two brothers. One of them learns that her husband and three sons have been sent away and confined in a prison, and the other learns that one brother has died a prisoner in a Hospital and that the other is sick.

This poor creature obtained from me a promise that if she would bring to me one of our men who had both his legs shot off at Wild Cat, and is now a prisoner there, I would give her in exchange for him her sick brother. She says she will never let the Lincoln General have any peace until he gives her the prisoner and she will bring him to me. How devoted, how noble is woman!

Here is a poor, fragile girl, travelling on horseback over two hundred miles to procure the release of a brother from prison and she will succeed too, if she begs the Lincoln officer with such words and tears as she besieged me with.

How fearful will be the accountability of those who brought on this war.

Some new mode of torture, heretofore unknown in Hades, will be invented for their punishment.[1]

Kindhearted Colonel Rains eventually was rewarded with a brigadier general's commission on November 4, 1862. Then on December 31, 1862, at the battle of Murfreesboro, Tennessee, or Stone's River, General Rains, "while valiantly leading his brigade and far in front, was instantly killed amid a terrific fire—his horse, from which he fell, plunging into the lines of the enemy."

Commenting upon the character of Rains, a contemporary declared him to be "fearless."[2] This was true, not only in battle where he was shot through the heart, but in peace, when his warm, heartfelt humanity overruled the cold, impersonal policies and procedures of war.

William McCarter, of the 116th Pennsylvania Infantry, recalled his contact and conversation with "some 17 or 18 Rebel soldiers, including an officer," who had been captured during the evacuation of Warrenton, Virginia, in 1862. McCarter states that, "although prisoners of war in our hands, [they] were no way backward in expressing their Secesh principles, and their determination to stand by the Southern Flag if they ever had again an opportunity to do so."

While preparing to leave the area, McCarter paid one last visit to the Confederate prisoners, relating,

> I turned back, and walk[ed] up to this Rebel officer whose gentlemanly bearing and appearance struck me very much, but whose countenance indicated want and hunger. I inquired, How are you off for Coffee, to which he replied with a sickly smile, "Coffee, Coffee, I did not see it for 6 weeks before being taken prisoner, and since then I and my men have been furnished with only 4 small rations each." "Hard enough Old Boy," said I, and being pretty liberally supplied with the article just then myself, for my little bag contained nearly a pound of it.
>
> I emptied fully $^3/_4$ of the quantity into his cap, the only thing he had to hold it. He seemed very grateful and thanked me politely in genuine Southern style, and bidding him good-bye I hurried after my companions.[3]

Gifts presented by a soldier to his enemy were not limited to simply coffee or supplies, but at times were of a much greater monetary value. Confederate colonel Wharton J. Green of Henry A. Wise's Legion, was captured at the battle of Roanoake Island, North Carolina, fought on February 8, 1862. Green's 2nd Battalion of North Carolina troops lost heavily during the engagement and his captor proved to be Col. John Kurtz of the 23rd Massachusetts Infantry Regiment.

Colonel Green was paroled some three weeks after the battle. But "as a token of his esteem for the kind and courteous treatment he received at the hands of his captor," the Rebel officer "solicited the privilege of presenting to Col. Kurtz a pet stallion worth $500."[4]

Regarding prisons and prisoners, it is with "incarceration" that we normally define our mental and visual interpretations of what life was like for a Civil War captive. Much of this concept is based on reality, while some perceptions owe their origin to myth and to stereotypes as manifested by the diary of Lt. Col. Frank T. Bennett, of the 55th Pennsylvania Infantry.

Colonel Bennett was a prisoner of war in various Confederate prisons located in Charleston and Columbia, South Carolina. Captured on March 10, 1862, on Tyleu Island, he remained incarcerated until October 10,

1862, and would later be imprisoned at Libby Prison in Richmond, Virginia, from May 16 to October 8, 1864. While writing from a jail in Charleston, South Carolina, on March 18, 1862, Bennett mentions how on the way to the city they were treated kindly by various Rebel officers, who provided a tent, and who "had prepared and sent in to us an excellent meal of fresh meat, boiled ham, rice, coffee and beans."

Upon arriving at Charleston, however, Bennett was introduced to Confederate general Roswell Sabine Ripley, actually a native of Ohio, whom Bennett describes as abrupt and harsh in his manner toward them. The captive laments how he and his fellow prisoners "should have fared better in the hands of a native of the South," and mentions the friendliness and hospitality of Confederate colonel John Cunningham of the 17th South Carolina Regiment of militia at Charleston during the war. Cunningham states that he was "the John Cunningham who first introduced the bill of secession into the South Carolina legislature," from whom he and his fellow captives had "received so many civilities. I should like to meet under other circumstances."

Bennett's entry for May 1, 1862, tells of the vermin in the jail or cell; he says that "cockroaches in swarms made their appearance." In the same breath, however, the Union officer states that their sheriff, "Mr. Dingle," was

> a very pleasant gentlemanly man whose regular Sunday visits to us were received by us with pleasure. . . . I can remember him as a generous and chivalrous enemy, . . . very different from our . . . Ripley. In fact most of the officers I have met are such as I have ever desired to contend with, that I could fight and at the same time give the hand of friendship.

Bennett's remarks almost smacked of "copperheadism"; for May 19, 1862, he wrote,

> I have yet to see the evils of slavery, the sufferings of the slave, and their desire to be freed from their masters. These things I never did believe. . . . The slaves are better off than a great many of our white laborers. Their condition [is] preferable to that of pauper whites of New England.

On page twenty-five of his diary, written between the lines of his only available paper (a copy of G. W. Curtis's *Lotus-Eating: A Summer Book,* published in 1852) Bennett mentions a visit by the lieutenant, "who conducted us from Charleston hither. He is an elderly gentleman and very pleasant. An invitation to his place in Newberry District. I shall certainly take advantage of, if I ever find my way to this state after the close of the war."

For May 23, Bennett mentions the kindness of the corporal in charge—Cpl. Lemuel Keisler of Co. K, 20th South Carolina Infantry—stating:

> His conduct was so straight forward, and there showed such kind feelings to us, that I obtained his name. I desire to remember the man. If the Rebel Army had more of such men, of the sound head type, it would be invincible. Corporal Lemuel Keisler, Rocky Well, S.C.

In his diary entry dated May 30, Bennett speaks of "Col. Preston, A.A.G. C.S.A.," commander of the area. Though communication with the North had been severed at that time, Preston promised to supply Bennett and his men with needed clothes and a doctor. Bennett's June 13 entry describes Preston as a man who "shows a desire to make us comfortable . . . so far as possible, a gentleman in a word. . . . I am very much pleased with the Confederate officers I have met. They are much more considerate of the prisoners than our papers led me to expect."

A few days earlier, on June 4, Bennett wrote about how Colonel Preston had offered to let the Federal officer walk "out of the jail; if necessary for my health, under a proper guard. I feel very much obliged to him, but I can accept no favors."[5]

Confederate captain Edward Allen Hitchcock McDonald (of Gen. Turner Ashby's Virginia forces) on August 9, 1862, after the battle of Cedar Run, Virginia, was given the responsibility of escorting 400 Federal prisoners of war to Orange Courthouse. As they traveled through the night, one of the Yankees

> gave out, so Edward dismounted and let him have his horse. Others followed this example and soon more prisoners than captors were mounted. . . . Not a man to let his prisoners starve, Edward broke open a box car full of

supplies and fed his charges. . . . Finally he telegraphed for a train, loaded them on, and got rid of them in Gordonsville. At parting, they gave a vote of thanks to Captain McDonald and Company D, "for their gentle and gallant behavior."[6]

Years after the war, Federal surgeon F. G. Hickman of Vandalia, Illinois, wrote of prison hospital service in Nashville. He recalled a "young cavalryman" in the hospital for quite some time, "who was shot through both feet, whose home was in Columbia [Tennessee]. . . . I remember he was taken to the provost marshal's in a spring wagon, not being able to sit up in a buggy."

W. B. Gordon, the above-mentioned Rebel cavalryman who had served in the 6th Tennessee or "Wheeler's Cavalry," Co. E, had observed the postwar comments of Dr. Hickman, and reconstructed the incident:

> I am the cavalryman alluded to, and am glad of the opportunity to testify to the considerate and Christian treatment shown by Dr. Hickman to the wounded Confederates in the prison hospital at Nashville. I was there from June 9th to August 22d, 1863. Dr. Hickman did all in his power to alleviate the suffering and for the comfort of the sick and wounded under his care. He never permitted the nurses to mistreat prisoners if he knew it.
>
> I could give you several illustrations of his kindness, but one will suffice. When my friends went to the hospital for me to be paroled, Dr. Hickman said he would go to the Capitol, too. I was carried down stairs . . . and put in a spring wagon. We asked the Doctor to ride with us, but he declined, saying he would walk.
>
> When we arrived at the Capitol the Doctor was there. Col. Spaulding, the Provost Marshal, had gone to dinner, and we had to wait nearly or quite an hour for his return. During that time Dr. Hickman stood on the ground and held his umbrella to protect me from the sun. What other Surgeon, Federal or Confederate, would have done that for a private prisoner of war?[7]

After the war, John T. Sloan of New Haven, Connecticut, formerly a member of the 1st Light Battery of the Connecticut Volunteers, reconstructed an incident during the fight at Grimball's Landing, James Island, South Carolina, in July 1863:

> Six prisoners were brought through our lines . . . while we were drinking coffee. We asked them to have a drink, but at first they refused, fearing the coffee had been poisoned, but finally one plucked up courage to try a drink, and the others followed his example and got away with quite a lot of coffee.
>
> Comrade William Fowler offered one of the prisoners a fifty cent piece, telling him that he would be sent to prison, and some of the United States money would come handy to have. The man took the coin but only stared at the giver, acting as if too frightened to thank him. The Johnnies looked so lean, hungry and poorly clad that they excited the sympathy of the Battery boys, and caused them to make up a purse of silver for them amounting to several dollars. Some of the comrades divided their rations with them.[8]

Louis N. Boudrye, 5th New York Cavalry chaplain, who was captured at Monterey Pass, Pennsylvania, on July 5, 1863, "during Gen. Kilpatrick's raid on the Rebel train, retreating from Gettysburg," recalled his experiences as a prisoner of war in a letter dated the seventeenth:

> Monday evening, the 6th, after a dreary day of marching and fasting—for our rations were short and poor—the column had halted and the prisoners sought sleep on the soft grass. I had just fallen into a doze, when I was roused up by a strange voice, calling "Chaplain Fifth New York Cavalry."
>
> Looking up, I beheld a Rebel lieutenant with whom I had conversed a little during the day, who stepped up toward me with a cup of smoking hot coffee and a fine piece of warm bread. "There, chaplain, I thought you might be hungry, and brought you this for your supper."

I was quite overcome with gratitude at an act so unexpected and so rare, and my heart leapt up for joy, as at the
sight of the first flower of spring.

That, I think, was a noble man, though he was a
Rebel. . . .[9]

Capt. Thomas S. McCahan, of the 9th Pennsylvania Cavalry, mentioned in his diary for October 13, 1863, the capture of 3rd Alabama soldiers, "Capt. Jones and private McMullin of Company D," near Paint
Rock or Maysville, Alabama. A few days later, on the sixteenth, McCahan
mentions that he had "turned over" his prisoners that day. He recorded:

I never met a stranger that I thought more of than the
rebel Captain Jones, he did not care to leave us. I went to
the Officers Commissary, got him a nice lot of provisions.
Taking them into him he asked me to get him a pen and
ink. I did, and some paper and Envelopes, thinking he
wanted to write to his friends.

I waited until he wrote it, he handed it to me[,] taking
[it] I noticed he had not sealed it and said so to him. He
remarked that it was for me. I bid him good bye and left
Reading the letter. It was to any party capturing me (In
case I was captured) stating how I had treated him, asking
that I be treated the same, etc.[10]

Not long after the war, Capt. William Hyndman of Co. A, 4th Pennsylvania Cavalry, recalled his experiences at the battle of Sulphur Springs,
Virginia, fought on October 12, 1863. Captain Hyndman was severely
wounded during the engagement, "shot in the head with a rifle ball,"
which he states "entered my right ear, and . . . came out at the back of my
head." He fell insensible from his horse and was picked up later by "rebel
troops who gave him a little water," and took him into their lines, where he
observed "nearly 300 of our men whom the enemy had captured."

On the way to Libby Prison in Virginia, Hyndman recounted an experience he and his fellow prisoners had at the hands of "the bitterest rebels,
the most inveterate foes to the Union cause . . . a South Carolina battalion
. . . , composed entirely of South Carolinians," about whom he states:

Who if they were rebels, proved themselves to be also men, they literally threw their whole supply of rations to us, cutting the sacks of hard-tack off the tops of their caissons, and throwing them wholesale into our midst, alongside the road. We thus had plenty for the time being. There were so many of us, though, that it did not last long. We received no more during the next two days.

This act of the South Carolinians was prompted by a pure spirit of humanity and generosity. The evening previous, too, while I could scarcely move, a Lieutenant of rebel infantry came and offered religious consolation. He actually knelt in prayer, and asked Divine mercy and aid for us all. This was a beautiful trait in the stern soldier, behind whose weather-beaten features, were the pulsations of a warm and Christian heart. . . . The remarks of this Christian Southerner were not at all insulting to the cause, but only tended purely to our spiritual welfare.

Incidents such as this prove that there were those in the rebel armies that were actuated by higher motives than demoniac revenge. . . .[11]

In February 1864, newspapers carried the account of the amiable friendship that developed when the 31st Ohio and the 54th Virginia Infantry regiment, their prisoners, aided one another. The narrative relates that

a few months ago the 31st Ohio, belonging to Streight's command, entered a town en route for Richmond, prisoners of war. Worn down, famished, hearts heavy and haversacks light, they were herded like dumb, driven cattle, to wear out the night.

A rebel regiment, the 54th Virginia, being camped near by, many of its men came strolling about to see the sorry show of poor supperless Yankees. They did not stare long, but hastened away to camp, and came streaming back with coffee kettle, corn bread and bacon, the best they had and all they had. . . .

Loyal guests and rebel hosts were mingled . . . and for that one night our common humanity stood acquitted of the heavy charge of total depravity with which it is blackened. . . . The prisoners in due time were exchanged. . . . But often, around the camp fires, I have heard them talk of the 54th Virginia, that proved themselves so immeasurably better "than a brother afar off," heard them wonder where they were, and discuss the chance that they might ever meet. . . .

And now comes the sequel that makes a beautiful poem of the whole of it. On the day of the storming of Mission Ridge, among the prisoners was the 54th Virginia, and on Friday it trailed away across the pontoon bridge and along the mountain road, nine miles to Kelley's Ferry. . . . A week elapsed and your correspondent followed suit. The Major of the 31st Ohio welcomed me to the warm hospitalities of his quarters and almost the first thing he said was, "you should have been here last Friday. . . . Will you believe the 54th Virginia has been here! Some of our boys were on duty at the landing when it arrived.

What regiment is this? they asked; and when the reply was given, they started for camp like quarter horses, and shouted, as they rushed in and out among the smoky cones of the Sibleys—the 54th Virginia is at the Ferry! The camp swarmed in three minutes. Treasures of coffee, bacon, sugar, beef, preserved peaches, everything, were turned out in force. . . . The same old scene, and yet how strangely changed. The twinkling fires, the grateful incense, the hungry captives; but guests and hosts had changed places; the star-lit folds floated aloft for the bonny blue flag; a debt of honor was paid to the uttermost farthing. . . .

And yet, should the 54th Virginia return to-morrow, with arms in their hands, to the Tennessee, the 31st Ohio would meet them on the bank, fight them foot to foot, and beat them back with rain so pitiless that the river would run red![12]

Contrary to popular opinion, not all guards in such notorious prisons as Camp Sumter or Andersonville were demonic persons hell-bent on destroying as many of their Federal prisoners as possible. Present at Andersonville in September 1864 was Samuel F. Mayes, formerly of Co. D, 7th Georgia Infantry, C.S.A., who had been wounded at both the First and Second Manassas, or Bull Run, in Virginia. He was later appointed sub-enrolling officer of the 8th Congressional District, Cobb County, Georgia, and had thus been placed in the 2nd Georgia Infantry of the Confederate army.

While stationed at Andersonville Prison as a guard, on September 20, 1864, he was surprisingly offered a gift by nine Federal prisoners. Their letter, signed and addressed to the then Lieutenant Mayes, states:

> Sir—We, the undersigned prisoners of war, now confined in the Confederate prison for upwards of eleven months, now deem it our duty to present you with a small and trifling testimonial to show you that we appreciate your noble and charitable conduct toward our poor sick brothers as well as the well ones.
>
> This watch that we present you with is not as noble as our hearts would be willing to present you with, but it is the best we are able to find. Hoping you may always be able to wear it in remembrance of those Federal prisoners who present you with it; hoping we may be able to enjoy the blessings of a peaceful and happy home, and meet as brothers and not as enemies in a very short time. Believe us, Lieutenant, to be your humble donors.[13]

In 1907 Samuel F. Mayes was living in Marietta, Georgia, and through the instrumentality of the United Daughters of the Confederacy released the above letter to the press, which he considered to be "one of his most precious possessions."

Not long after the above event, Pvt. George W. Potter, of Co. F, 2nd Tennessee Infantry (U.S.A.), escaped from Andersonville Prison and made his way to Chattanooga. Potter had originally been captured after the engagement at Rogersville, Tennessee, on November 6, 1863. He was first taken to Belle Isle Prison on the James River near Richmond, Virginia, but eventually was transferred along with other Federal prisoners to

Andersonville in March 1864, where he remained in the hospital for a considerable time.

By early 1865, a number of prisoners had successfully escaped the famous compound, "by climbing the fence around the prison." Potter was one of these fortunate individuals, but while on the road, not far from the prison he

> . . . met a rebel soldier who immediately recognized him, but informed him that he would do him no harm. The man kept him concealed for three days while the weather was bad, gave him a supply of privisions, and a map of the country, and started him off. . . .[14]

Writing from his headquarters near Savannah, Georgia, to his wife Ella, on December 30, 1864, Col. Thomas J. Jordan of the 9th Pennsylvania Cavlary sent a letter received from a Confederate prisoner named John W. Smith, incarcerated at Camp Chase, Ohio. Jordan explains that he captured the Rebel soldier at McMinnville, Tennessee, who

> was about to be killed by some of the 5th Tennessee Cavalry who I had with me, when I rescued him from them and had him sent safely to Tullehomma [sic]. His letter shows that he has a heart. I will answer it, if only to help him wile away a weary hour in his prison.

The letter from Smith, dated December 9, states,

> Dear Sir, I take my pen in hand this morning to return you my sincere and unfeigned thanks for your kind and considerate treatment toward me while I was a prisoner in your charge. . . . I am very thankful and if I should ever be so fortunate as to be exchanged and capture any of them or you or any of your regiment I will remember them for it. . . . If you see lieutenant Smith of the 4th Tenn cav who you sent me to Tullahoma by, give him my respects and tell him that I would consider it quite an honor to meet him either at home in peace or on the field of Battle.[15]

Confederate captain James M. Winston (of the 12th Mississippi Cavalry) was noted as a kind and sympathetic man, even toward his enemies during the war. After the war, a daughter recalled an incident when his command had "captured a squad of Federal soldiers," containing one individual who limped badly "from a sprained ankle." Winston told one of his men to dismount and let the wounded man ride. "Why, Captain," the man replied, "he is a Yankee; make him walk." Winston emphatically declared, "Dismount, sir, and put that crippled man on your horse. Never strike a man when he is down, even if he is a foe."

On another occasion Captain Winston once again had captured a number of Union soldiers, the captain of which came up to him and offered his watch and roll of greenbacks. The Rebel officer replied, "Put your watch and money back in your pocket. I am a soldier, not a robber."[16]

A touching story of compassion concerns that of Pvt. Harvey Grubb of the 22nd Pennsylvania Volunteer Cavalry, whose regiment was "kept almost constantly in the saddle, and was exposed to great hardships and privations, in moving over mountain roads covered with ice and snow and swept by wintry blasts."[17] During the years of 1863 and 1864, the regiment was active in the mountains of West Virginia and the Shenandoah Valley of Virginia, capturing bands of Confederate soldiers at times. A descendant of Grubb describes that the cavalryman

> had been out on a slippery, icy night in the Shenandoah Valley of Virginia; men were falling down. The Twenty-second were bringing a number of Confederate prisoners back to camp. The column of prisoners balked, however, and wouldn't go forward.
>
> Grubb couldn't understand what the holdup was, so he spurred his horse forward through the prisoners and found they were stopping at an icy stream they didn't want to cross. (He was thinking at the time of his brother, who had supposedly died in a Rebel prison, but actually was at Camp Parole, Maryland, at Annapolis, where he recuperated.)
>
> Grubb took a Rebel prisoner, set him on a rock or tree stump and handed him his own musket or rifle, though he still retained his side arm pistol. He told the soldier, "Don't move off that rock or I'll have to kill you." Next

he took each of the prisoners or the "walking wounded" in turn, put them on his back or horse, and got them across the icy stream so they didn't have to wade through the frigid waters.[18]

One of the most extraordinary accounts concerning the humanity shown toward enemy prisoners occurred after the battle of Glasgow, Missouri, fought on October 15, 1864. The Federal garrison under the command of Col. Chester Harding, Jr., of the 43rd Missouri Volunteer Infantry, surrendered to a brigade of the Confederate army, commanded by John B. Clark.

On the day after the surrender, Colonel Harding and the officers of his command, "numbering twenty-eight in all," were marched toward the Federal post at Boonville, some thirty miles away. Their escort consisted of Co. H, 3rd Missouri Mounted Infantry, C.S.A., numbering forty-nine rank and file, under the command of Lt. James W. Graves.

Prior to the battle of Glasgow, notorious bands of guerrillas prowled throughout the neighborhood committing a number of atrocious acts against their victims, including the scalping of unarmed Federal troops. The most nefarious band was that of "Bloody Bill" Anderson who, according to the following account, was supported by Gen. Joseph O. Shelby, whose artillery had operated during the attack on Glasgow.

The terms of surrender, agreed upon between Clark and Harding, were that "the Federal officers and enlisted men should be parolled and permitted to return to their homes, there to remain until duly exchanged." Gen. William S. Rosecrans of the Federal army, however, had refused to recognize any paroles as binding upon any of his captured officers unless delivered to the nearest Union military post, "to be there certified as paroled." Consequently, Lieutenant Graves and his men were forced to remove their prisoners to the Federal post at Boonville, Missouri.

During the march, Lieutenant Graves had taken the precaution of throwing out flankers and an advanced guard. The sergeant of the advance returned and reported that 100 or more men, "seemingly Federal Cavalry," were halted at the forks of the road half a mile ahead. Though they wore Federal uniforms, the sergeant had observed through his field glass that they were in reality "Bloody Bill" Anderson's gang of guerrillas, who had followed them in an attempt to "take the prisoners from the escort, and murder and rob them."

Lieutenant Graves soon formed a line of battle, and addressed his men in the following manner:

> Men, you are Confederate soldiers. Anderson and his gang are but robbers and cutthroats who dishonor our colors. I have served in the ranks with you for three years, and I need not ask you if you will do your duty.

The orderly sergeant answered, "Lieutenant, you can bet your life on the men. They will stand by you, and defend the prisoners to the death." The whole company responded, "Aye, to the death."

Turning to the Federal officers, Lieutenant Graves said: "Gentlemen, you have heard my statement, and understand the emergency that we are to face, if I do not mistake the purpose of the miscreants in my front. I shall advance at all hazards, but do not feel warranted in taking you under fire without your free consent. *You need not consider yourselves prisoners any longer,* should you wish to retire and make the effort to reach Boonville by another road. *I have 12 extra rifles in the wagons, with plenty of ammunition,* that I brought along expecting to secure some recruits before rejoining my command. *You can have them, and I can supply you also with 10, 44 calibre revolvers.*"

Not surprisingly, the Federal prisoners voted to stand with Lieutenant Graves and his men, "not as prisoners but as American soldiers, and the Confederates as comrades in arms." The Federal soldiers took their positions in line, while the others rendered service "by acting as horse-holders."

While the arms were being distributed to the Union soldiers, four men from Anderson's guerrilla force advanced on the road to Graves's position, carrying a white flag. Lieutenant Graves rode out to meet them, accompanied by six of his own soldiers. Within some four or five yards of the enemy, he halted and demanded to know who they were and their intentions. They informed him that they were indeed a portion of Colonel Anderson's cavalry as had been suspected. They remarked:

> "We want those Yankee officers you've got along with you. They are the ones that butchered some of our men at Palmyra. They belong to McNeil's Brigade, and Col. Anderson says if you refuse to give 'em up he will take 'em any how. He has 300 men with him, and you can

save trouble by giving up the Yanks. They're our meat and we're going to have 'em for sure."

Lieutenant Graves replied, "Tell Bill Anderson that his damnable proposal is too infamous for me to consider for an instant. We are Confederate soldiers, and he and his men are murderers and thieves. Tell him if he does not get away from my line of march, and clear out with his gang of cut throats in five minutes, I will open fire upon him. Now, be off quick and not another word from you. You deserve to be hanged for bringing such a proposition."

Graves returned, told what had been said. He found that twenty-two Federal officers who were armed had formed on the left of the line, and he requested them to take position at the center, saying, "Gentlemen, I desire you to be where we can guard both your flanks."

A captain of the Federal prisoners had hid his company flag underneath his overcoat when captured, and now asked permission to display it. Consent was given,

> and the flag, attached to an improvised staff, waved side by side with the Confederate battle flag, a red St. Andrew's cross on a blue field. . . . It was indeed an extraordinary command—a Confederate-Federal company of veterans of both great armies. Nothing could have been more incongruous tested by the laws of war, and yet nothing was more natural than the spectacle of American soldiers in the same line of battle advancing against a common enemy. . . .

The men were equipped with Winchester repeating rifles and Springfield breechloaders, while ten of the Federal officers had Colt revolvers issued to them. Night fell, and "a double line of sentinels was posted," composed of both Federal soldiers and Confederates. The next morning the force was met by a detail of Union cavalry from Boonville. Gen. W. S. Rosecrans later met Lieutenant Graves at Lexington, Missouri, and thanked him for his display of honor and civility to his captured foe.

Years after the war, the Federal officers who literally owed Graves their lives located him residing with his family in western Texas. He met his former prisoners at St. Louis, where they "presented him a massive gold medal of elegant design, bearing upon one of its faces two clasped hands, beneath the flag of the Union, and on the other an inscription referring to the event that the medal was designed to commemorate."[19]

In substantiation of Lt. James W. Graves's humanitarianism toward his enemy, Col. Chester Harding, Jr., of the 43rd Missouri Federal Infantry, filed an official report of the battle of Glasgow and his subsequent surrender to General Clark. He stated:

> We were treated with courtesy and kindness by General Clark and nearly all of the officers whom we came in contact with. I desire particularly to acknowledge the assiduous care which Lieutenant Graves, of the Third (rebel) Missouri Volunteers, commanding our escort, bestowed upon us and the good behavior of his men. Had they been our own troops we could not have been better treated.[20]

Such amiable treatment as expressed above would continue to be manifested in both word and deed to the war's end and beyond.

CHAPTER 7

Friends at the Bitter End

THE YEAR 1865 USHERED IN THE BEGINNING OF THE END FOR THE Confederate States of America. Though Capt. James I. Waddell of the *Shenandoah,* the Confederate privateer, would continue to attack U.S. whaling vessels in the Arctic waters of the Bering Strait as late as June 28, and Cherokee Confederate general Stand Watie would not surrender until June 23, for all intents and purposes the Southern fight for independence was over by April 9 when Gen. Robert E. Lee surrendered the Army of Northern Virginia to Gen. Ulysses S. Grant at Appomattox Courthouse, Virginia.

Hunter Marshall, a corporal of the "Beauregard Rifles" in Shoemaker's Lynchburg (Virginia) Battery of the "Stuart Horse Artillery," recalled that on Friday, the seventh of April,

> our Army was in a dreadful condition and we realized the situation fully, as everything was on the ragged edge, there was no food for man nor beast and no prospect of getting any soon. . . . Saturday morning (on the eighth) early each man in my Company was given an ear of corn from a corn crib as his ration for the day and this was the last ration that I received from the confederate govern-ment.[1]

Norfleet Saunders Smith, a captain in the 3rd North Carolina Cavalry (C.S.A.), who commanded the "Scotland Neck Mounted Riflemen," was "given the credit for the last cavalry charge of the war near Appomattox the day before General Lee surrendered." His daughter recalled that her father "had a great big black horse named FOSSET. At Appomattox, the night before Lee surrendered, Fosset laid down on Papa's sword and broke it in half. He said he knew then the war was over because Fosset had broken the sword."[2]

The events of the surrender are almost beyond belief as they exemplified the acts of compassion and lack of animosity expressed by the opposing armies and their leaders. As Seth M. Flint of the 5th U.S. Cavalry later remembered,

> I had been in fifteen or sixteen battles during three years, and had come to have a wholesome esteem for the Johnny rebs and their leader. . . . What a brave pair of thorough breds Lee and Traveler were! That horse would have attracted attention anywhere. . . . General Lee's uniform was immaculate and he presented a superb martial figure.
>
> But it was the face beneath the gray felt hat and hair that made the deepest impression on me; I say this because I can still recall it vividly. I have been trying to find a single word that describes it, and I have concluded that "benign" is the adjective I am after; because that means kindly, gracious, and despite its sternness on that day of long ago, I would still call his expression benign. . . . How Abe Lincoln would have enjoyed that confab! Like Grant, he would have grasped the hands of those soldiers in Confederate gray and welcomed them back home. Had he been spared, there would have been no Reconstruction.[3]

On Palm Sunday, April 9, 1865, Gen. Robert E. Lee, realizing that surrender was imminent, allegedly remarked, "There is nothing left me but to go and see General Grant, and I would rather die a thousand deaths."[4] Yet the Union commander's demands of surrender were anything but horrendous or demoralizing to Lee and his half-starved army. Grant's conditions graciously "gave the officers their sidearms, private horses, and personal baggage," so that the defeated rebels could "go home and go to work, and the government would not throw any obstacles in the way." Lee accepted the terms and commented how such generosity "would have a most happy effect."

Grant recounted that at the McLean House "Lee no doubt expected me to ask for his sword, but I did not want his sword, and while smiling, commented to the defeated Confederate that it would only have gone to the Patent Office to be worshiped by the Washington rebels." Grant stated to Lee that he saw "the wisdom of these men getting home and to work as soon as possible," and gave orders "to allow any soldier or officer claiming a horse or mule to take it. General Lee showed some emotion at this—a feeling which I also shared—and said it would have a most happy effect. The interview ended, I gave orders for rationing his troops."[5]

Gen. Robert E. Lee appears never to have forgotten the kind, conciliatory actions of Grant at Appomattox that April day in 1865. After the war Lee accepted a position as the president of Washington College. On one occasion a faculty member spoke critically of Ulysses S. Grant, after which Lee, generally a kind, soft-spoken person, rebuked the man with harsh words: "Sir, if you presume ever again to speak disrespectfully of General Grant in my presence, either you or I will sever his connection with this University."[6]

At Appomattox there were no cheers of humiliation shouted at the defeated Confederate forces, neither were there fired victory volleys by gun or cannon. At one point after the surrender, there was an attempt of a "firing of 100 guns in token of victory," but General Grant "quickly stopped it."[7] As the defeated Rebel troops marched through the streets of Appomattox, Union officer Joshua Chamberlain of Maine, and of the battle of Gettysburg fame, "ordered a salute to the Rebel banners." Chamberlain recalled:

> Before us in proud humiliation stood . . . men whom neither toils and sufferings, nor the fact of death, nor disaster could bend their resolve; standing before us now, thin, worn and famished, but erect, and with eyes looking level into ours, waking memories that bound us together as no other bond.

As the Rebel troops marched by, they in turn saluted the Union forces, and Chamberlain once again remembered:

On our part not a sound of trumpet more, nor roll of
drum; not a cheer, nor word nor whisper . . . nor motion
. . . but an awed stillness rather, and breath-holding, as if
it were the passing of the dead.

As each . . . division halts, the men face inwards to-
wards us across the road, twelve feet away . . . worn and
half-starved as they were . . . they fix bayonets, stack
arms. . . . Lastly—reluctantly, with agony of expression—
they tenderly fold the flags, battle-worn and torn, blood-
stained, heart-holding colors, and lay them down; some
frenziedly rushing from the ranks, kneeling over them,
clinging to them, pressing them to their lips with burning
tears. . . .

How could we help falling on our knees, all of us together, and praying God to pity and forgive us all![8]

On May 9, 1865, famed cavalry officer Lt. Gen. Nathan Bedford For-
rest sent a memo from Gainesville, Alabama, addressed to the soldiers
under his command, stating:

The armies of Generals Lee and Johnston having surrendered, you are the last of all the troops of the C.S. Army
east of the Mississippi River to lay down your arms. . . .
The Government which we sought to establish and per-
petuate is at an end. Reason dictates and humanity de-
mand that no more blood be shed. . . . It is your duty and
mine to lay down our arms, submit to the "powers that
be," and to aid in restoring peace and establishing law
and order throughout the land. The terms upon which
you were surrendered are favorable, and should be satis-
factory and acceptable to all. They manifest a spirit of
magnanimity and liberality on the part of the Federal au-
thorities which should be met on our part by a faithful
compliance with all the stipulations and conditions
therein expressed. As your commander, I sincerely hope
that every officer and soldier of my command will cheerfully obey the orders and carry out in good faith all the
terms of the cartel. . . .

Civil war, such as you have just passed through, naturally engenders feelings of animosity, hatred, and revenge. It is our duty to divest ourselves of all such feelings, and so far in our power to do so to cultivate friendly feelings toward those with whom we have so long contested and heretofore so widely but honestly differed. Neighborhood feuds, personal animosities, and private differences should be blotted out, and when you return home a manly, straightforward course of conduct will secure the respect even of your enemies. Whatever your responsibilities may be to Government, to society, or to individuals, meet them like men. . . .

You have been good soldiers, you can be good citizens. Obey the laws, preserve your honor, and the Government to which you have surrendered can afford to be and will be magnanimous.[9]

At the end of the Civil War, famed Federal army nurse Clara Barton journeyed south to the infamous Confederate prison camp known as Andersonville, where some 13,000 Union troops had perished. Here she was successful in identifying and marking many of the graves of the deceased soldiers. In a report dated March 1866, she mentions the "humane public-spirited citizen of Fort Valley, Georgia," referred to simply as "Mr. Griffin."

Mr. Griffin, along with twenty of "the ever-faithful negroes," had been responsible for reinterring the bodies of dead Federals, whose remains "were rooted up by animals." Gen. James A. Wilson appointed Griffin as the "temporary Superintendent" of the former prison camp's cemetery and provided him with limited means to accomplish his humanitarian task. Actually, according to Miss Barton, Griffin had himself "furnished the labor at his own cost, while General Wilson issued the necessary rations."

Interestingly, Mr. Griffin was none other than Col. Joel R. Griffin, formerly of the 8th Georgia Cavalry (C.S.A.), who gave testimony after the war at the trial of Capt. Henry Wirz, commandant at Andersonville. Griffin, of the Army of Northern Virginia, stated how he had specifically gone to Andersonville in an attempt "to improve and beautify" the cemetery, and to

cover the bodies that had been somewhat exposed which I did. I found the graveyard in rather a bad condition. It had been disturbed by cows, and part of the graves torn

up to some extent, which I had covered. Two of the bodies were exposed; the bodies were placed in lines, and the
dirt having been in some instances taken off them in part,
the graves were somewhat offensive; that is, of the last
bodies buried. No measure had been taken by the rebel
government to care for that graveyard that I know of.

I saw no reason at all to believe that the uncovering of
those bodies was intentional; it was from want of care.
That was three or four weeks probably, after the Andersonville prison had been broken up.[10]

The significant point here is that even though the Civil War had literally ended only days earlier, a former Confederate officer carefully and car-
ingly took it upon himself to honor the enemy dead by providing them
proper burial. The wounds of a war, in which over 600,000 individuals lost
their lives, had already begun to heal.

Many miles to the northeast of Andersonville lies the grave of a Federal
soldier, Sgt. Jerome Pierce of the 36th Massachusetts Infantry, killed at the
battle of the Bloody Angle in Virginia on May 12, 1864. His body was
later removed to the National Cemetery at Fredericksburg where, ever
since, a Southern family has continually decorated the grave of this Yankee
soldier. Several years after the war, Pierce's descendants sent $100 to care
for their relative's grave. A fund was begun at a local bank and, from that
time to the present, the remains of a Northern soldier have been perpetu-
ally honored and remembered. As an elderly Virginian, Mrs. Alice Heflin
Abernathy commented, "it never made any difference to us that he was a
Yankee—never even thought about it."[11]

Just as Confederate colonel Joel R. Griffin had buried the Union dead
at Andersonville, a sexton and ex-slave, John W. Jones, formerly of Lees-
burg, Virginia, interred (at the Government's expense), the majority of
Rebel dead at Woodlawn Cemetery, individuals who died at the infamous
Elmira Prison in Chemung County, New York. As one author stated,
"Here were laid 2,988 of the prisoners . . . There is something rather sug-
gestive in the fact that the last rites of so many of those who had been enlisted in an effort to preserve slavery as an institution of their country
should have been performed by one who had escaped from slavery."[12]

Thus humanitarian acts were at times both "color-blind" and without
guile, as well as ideologically and politically irrelevant both during the war
and after its end.

CHAPTER 8

A Brotherhood for the Enemy

IN LATE DECEMBER 1849, AT NEW ORLEANS, THE HONORABLE S. S. Prentiss offered a toast at the "Celebration of the Landing of the Pilgrims," stating: "The Union—May it be perpetual. May the time never arrive when a son of New England shall be a foreigner in New Orleans, or a Creole a foreigner in New England."[1]

Yet, contrary to the wishes of Prentiss, John A. Tainter of Hartford, Connecticut, dying in 1862, left all his property—amounting close to one million dollars—to his wife and two daughters upon certain conditions. In his will he forbade "either of his daughters to marry a foreigner, or a native of a Southern or slaveholding State, under penalty of forfeiting her interest in the property."[2]

During the war, Federal private Frank Wilkeson was serving at Stevenson, Alabama, in a refugee camp that aided women and children who had been driven from their homes or starved out in the Appalachian Mountain region. Here he was told of their homes being burned, of crops ruined, and of husbands murdered. Gathering their children around them, Wilkeson recounted:

> I heard them repeat over and over to their children the names of men which they were never to forget, and whom they were to kill when they had sufficient strength to hold a rifle. . . . These women, who had been driven from their homes by the most savage warfare our country has been cursed with, knew what war was, and they impressed me as living wholly to revenge their wrongs.[3]

Fortunately, such accounts were the exception rather than the rule. The majority of soldiers and civilians, "pulled themselves up by their boot strings," and carried on as best they could under trying circumstances. Though fortunes were lost and times were hard, families persevered through the period known as the "Reconstruction" and beyond, regardless of the activities of the Ku Klux Klan or northern carpetbaggers.

Perhaps a Southern artilleryman, describing the aftermath of a battle during the war, aptly summarized with vivid imagery the forlorn and pathetic condition with which both man and beast were forced to contend at the conflict's end:

> When the firing ceased an old battery horse, his lower jaw carried away by a shot, with blood streaming from his wound, staggered up to him, gazed beseechingly at him, and, groaning piteously, laid his bloody jaws on his shoulder, and so made his appeal for sympathy.[4]

Such heartrending circumstances, regardless of the "waving of the bloody shirt" by politicians, helped the majority of Americans soon after the war to once again become brothers, fellow citizens, despite the "fanaticism of a few zealots at the North or a few hot heads at the South."[5] The triumphant march of Gilbert H. Bates, formerly of Co. H, 1st Wisconsin Volunteers, throughout the Southern states in 1868 revealed that a former Union soldier, carrying the American flag, alone and unarmed, could also go unmolested through former "enemy" territory.[6]

The oft-repeated "baptism by fire, blood, and sword," shared by the soldiers of both armies, without doubt greatly aided in bringing about their reconciliation toward one another, as witnessed by reunions held at Gettysburg and elsewhere long after the war. Under the headline, "Old Enemies Fraternizing," national newspapers in May 1883 carried the details of a reunion held at Niagara Falls by members of the former 28th New York Infantry Regiment and the former Confederate 5th Virginia Infantry of the "Stonewall Brigade."

The former Confederate veterans and their Union counterparts were escorted to the Prospect Park pavilion by the Sprout and Dudley Posts of the G.A.R. (Grand Army of the Republic Veteran organization), composed of former Federal soldiers. The 5th Virginia veterans brought with them to the twenty-second annual reunion "the flag they captured from the New

York 28th at the battle of Cedar Mountain, August 9, 1862," which they returned to the Union veterans during the ceremonies:

> The Virginia Regiment was welcomed by Captain Flagler, President of the Twenty-Eighth Regiment Association, in an eloquent address. Captain Stickney, of the Virginians, responded. Captain Bumgardner, of the Virginia regiment, presented to the Twenty-Eighth the flag captured by them during the War of the Rebellion. Col. E. F. Brown of the Twenty-Eighth, responded. . . .
>
> The best of feelings prevails, and the Southerners are in ecstasy over their treatment.[7]

Simultaneously, while former enemies met in New York as comrades in arms, forty-five veterans of the 100th and 131st Pennsylvania Regiments arrived at Fredericksburg, Virginia, on May 22, 1883, "to visit their old battlefields. They were hospitably received by the Maury Camp of Confederate Veterans and cordially welcomed by the citizens generally."[8]

During the following year, Confederate veteran Robert E. Lee Camp No. 1, commanded by the mayor of Richmond, Virginia, William C. Carrington, extended "the right hand of friendship and fellowship to their late adversaries." Conjointly, with the Phil Kearny Post No. 10, of the G.A.R., department of Virginia, they had

> decorated Confederate soldiers' graves at Hollywood cemetery and Union soldiers' graves at Richmond National cemetery; have received and entertained a large delegation of the members of the Pennsylvania legislature, a majority of whom belong to the G.A.R. have received and entertained Lincoln Post, No. 11, G.A.R., Newark, N.J.; will receive and entertain in connection with Phil Kearny Post the veterans of the Sixty-first Pennsylvania Volunteers, who visit Richmond for the purpose of observing the anniversary of the battle of Fair Oaks, on the 31st of May.

It is perhaps most significant to note, that the former Confederate and Union soldiers were also proposing to hold "a grand fair the latter part of February and during the month of March, in order to raise a fund to carry

"Comrades." Civil War Veterans Reunion at Gettysburg, 1913. COURTESY OF THE HISTORICAL SOCIETY OF PENNSYLVANIA, PHILADELPHIA.

out their benevolent mission." This "mission" was to specifically assist the sick "and disabled comrades of the late Confederate army and their families, many of whom are in dire need, to establish a soldier's home for their indigent and infirm veterans."[9]

During the famous "Gettysburg Reunion" held in 1913 at the former battlefield, two veterans of that engagement—and former enemies—met one another once again, but under much different circumstances. Participating in the famed Pickett's Charge in July 1863, A. C. Smith of the 56th Virginia Infantry had actually "just climbed over" the wall "when he was hit" by a Federal bullet. He told friends at the wall in 1913 that after being wounded "a Union soldier gave him some water and took him to the hospital," adding, "He's gone to his reward by this time I reckon."

At that moment, Albert N. Hamilton, a veteran of the 72nd Pennsylvania Infantry, arrived at the same wall, and was telling his friends that "it was right here that a Johnny fell into my arms. I lifted him up and gave him a swig of water, and then got him on my shoulders and carried him off, but. . . ." At that instance, Smith, who'd been listening, called out to Hamilton and shouted, "Praise the Lord! Praise the Lord, it's YOU, brother!" Then the two former foes are said to have "fell into each other's arms, embracing."[10]

After the war, congeniality and friendship were not expressed solely by former soldiers who had fought against one another, but also extended to civilians and their former enemies. One touching incident was recorded by Thomas G. Jones, former major in the Army of Northern Virginia, and governor of the State of Alabama from 1890 to 1894.

In April 1874, Jones was the speaker for "Confederate Memorial Day" held at Montgomery, Alabama. During his remarks he spoke "kindly words for those who fell on the other side, and expressed himself eloquently and feelingly in favor of reconciliation." Unknown to Jones, a widow in New York would read his remarks and, though withholding her name, forwarded to the former Confederate officer a letter and special gift. She wrote:

> The war widowed me and took away my two sons. For a long time I felt as if I could never forgive those who slew the defenders of the "stars and stripes," but when I think of the war-widowed mothers of the South, and see such language as this, it makes me tenderer and juster to the South.
>
> I feel that men like this Major Jones must be noble and true in heart, and fought and died because they thought it was right. I want them to feel that such sentiments echo in the Northern heart, and in truth tend to draw the whole country together for its sealing.[11]

Along with the above letter, the widowed mother sent to Major Jones an inscribed silver cup that she had commissioned a jewelry firm to send. The inscription read as follows:

To
Major Thomas G. Jones
The Orator on Confederate Memorial Day
April, 1874;
from
A Northern woman, widowed and bereft

of her two sons by the War,
As a token of her appreciation of the
Soldierly words, spoken in kindness of
The Northern Dead.

The article containing the above account declared that such incidents "will tend more toward bringing about a healthy feeling of kindness between North and South than all the formal reconciliations that officious and ingenious minds can devise."[12] This feeling had been echoed during the war as well, in 1862, when Confederate prisoners at Huntsville, Alabama, were permitted by their Federal commandant to hold ceremonial services for a deceased comrade. The soldiers remarked to their warden that they hoped such a courtesy might create in the not too distant future, a day

> when the soldiers of the South and the defenders of the
> Union could shake hands and fight by each other's side in
> a common cause. The moral effect of such an event is
> greater than that of a battle. With this war brought to a
> close, how many a thousand will exclaim: "Oh that we
> had known each other better before."[13]

Of course, former Yankee and Rebel soldiers would indeed get their opportunity to fight together in a common cause in the country's next conflict, the Spanish-American War, fought at the end of the nineteenth century. The first martyr at that time would be a white Southerner, Worth Bagley from North Carolina. The *Atlanta Constitution* described Bagley as a martyr whose blood had been "spilled upon his country's altar," thus sealing "effectively the covenant of brotherhood between the north and south," and completing "the work of reconciliation which commenced at Appomattox." The *New York Tribune* simultaneously declared Bagley's death as "the first sacrifice of the war. There is no north and no south after that, we are all Worth Bagley's countrymen."[14]

Intense and emotionally charged conflicts such as a vicious and devastating war can, ironically, both create as well as destroy. Bruce Catton, the late eminent Civil War historian, related the words of a survivor of the Army of the Cumberland: "None of us were fond of war; but there had grown up between the boys an attachmant for each other they never had nor ever will have for any other body of men."[15]

This feeling of brotherhood or comradeship in battle is aptly summarized by Shakespeare in the words he attributes to King Henry V during the conflict with the French at the battle of Agincourt in 1415:

> "We few, we happy few, we band of brothers,
> For he today that sheds his blood with me,
> Shall be my brother, Be he neer so vile,
> This day shall gentle his condition."[16]

Though Rebels and Yankees served on opposing sides and differed in cultural, political, or economic ideologies, they simultaneously sweated, starved, bled, and died under markedly similar conditions—becoming, in effect, brothers in battle. Perhaps Oliver Wendell Holmes summarized most appropriately the basis for mutual respect repeatedly shown by the one-time enemies toward one another, both during and after the American Civil War:

> You could not stand up day after day in those indecisive
> contests, where overwhelming victory was impossible be-
> cause neither side would run as they ought when beaten,
> without getting at least something of the same brother-
> hood for the enemy that the north pole of a magnet has
> for the south.[17]

Though the American Civil War ended almost 150 years ago, it has continued to capture the imagination of scholars and the public alike. With the popularity of reenactment groups and the continued publication of numerous books and articles, interest in the subject appears to be in no way waning. Professional historians will, of course, continue to debate the causes and origins of the war for years to come. Yet the stories of brotherhood between North and South demonstrate a verity of human nature gleaned from the conflict and its participants—noble virtues that personified to a marked degree both the officer and the private during the Civil War, whether Union or Confederate.

This truth is best summarized by the words of poet Henry Wadsworth Longfellow: "The bravest are the tenderest. The loving are the daring."

Note: "HSP" is the Historical Society of Pennsylvania in Philadelphia.

INTRODUCTION

1. Hans Delbruck, *History of the Art of War*, trans. Walter J. Renfroe, Jr. (Westport, Conn.: Greenwood, 1982), 3: 211.
2. Grant Uden, *A Dictionary of Chivalry* (Harmondsworth, England: Penguin Books, 1968), 126–27.
3. Gene DuVall, "A Most Memorable Christmas," *American Legion* (Dec. 1994): 24–25, 56.
4. John H. Moffit, "Kriegsfangenen" (Prisoner of war), manuscript in author's possession.
5. James Cornell Biddle, letters (1861–65) to his wife, Gertrude C. Meredith Biddle, box 1, collection no. 1881, HSP (hereafter cited as Biddle letters).
6. Ibid., Apr. 13, 1865.
7. Seth M. Flint and William Rose Lee, "I Saw Lee Surrender," *Saturday Evening Post* 212 (Apr. 6, 1940): 27, 87–90.
8. "A Strange Scene," *Forney's (Philadelphia) War Press*, Jul. 23, 1864, 3.
9. Kate Cumming, *A Journal of Hospital Life in the Confederate Army of Tennessee, from the Battle of Shiloh to the End of the War* (Louisville, Ky.: John P. Morton, 1866), 14.
10. "Yank and Johnny Reb," *Lewistown [Pa.] Gazette*, Apr. 29, 1897, 1, col. 3.

CHAPTER 1: FRATERNIZING WITH THE ENEMY

1. Barbour R. Rolph, correspondence with author, Jul. 24, 1980; *Presidents, Soldiers, Statesmen* (New York: H. H. Hardesty, 1889), 567–68.

2. Franklin Boyts, diary (1862–65), collection no. 1995, call no. AM .13752, vol. 7, HSP.

3. Oliver Hopkinson, letters (1861–63), "Autographs" in Hopkinson Papers, collection no. 1978, vol. 19 (Nov. 24, 1862), 14, HSP.

4. Stanley F. Horn, ed., *Tennessee's War, 1861–1865: Described by Participants* (Nashville: Tennessee Civil War Centennial Commission, 1965), 137.

5. Ibid., 157–58.

6. G. Earle Thompson, ed., "Diary of a Delaware Yank," typescript copy, Society Miscellaneous Collection, HSP.

7. Abraham Sturgis, Isaac Sturgis, and James Sturgis and William Sturgis, all of Smithfield, Fayette County, Pennsylvania, letters (1861–64), typescript, collection no. 831, call no. AM .2075, HSP, 75.

8. "Fraternizing of the Soldiers," *Philadelphia Public Ledger,* Jul. 24, 1863, 2, col. 1.

9. "Fraternization," *Forney's (Philadelphia) War Press,* Aug. 1, 1863, 8, col. 4.

10. John P. Green, "Personal Recollections of the Civil War," Dec. 1914, unprocessed collection, HSP, 90.

11. Henry Y. Warnock, ed., *Sound of Drums: Selected Writings of Spencer B. King* (Macon, Ga.: Mercer University Press, 1984), 296–97.

12. John L. Smith, Papers (book of mimeographed/carbon-copied Civil War letters [1862–65]; also miscellaneous loose original letters, diaries, letter books, etc.), Civil War letters (1862–1865), collection no. 610, HSP (hereafter cited as Smith Papers).

13. Ibid., 229–30.

14. Ibid., letter of Aug. 7, 1864.

15. Ibid., letter of Aug. 12, 1864.

16. David Coles and David W. Hartman, *Biographical Rosters of Florida's Confederates and Union Soldiers, 1861–1865* (Wilmington, N.C.: Broadfoot, 1995), 1: 199–200.

17. Smith Papers, 255–58.

18. Donald Lewis Osborn, *Knowing the Bruners* (Lee's Summit, Mo., 1968), 166.

19. John W. Mitchell, letter, Oct. 28, 1864, in William Frederick Allen Civil War Correspondence (1860–1865), incoming, collection no. 1919, HSP.

20. W. H. Tunnard, *A Southern Record: The History of the Third Regiment, Louisiana Infantry* (Baton Rouge, La., 1866), 305–7.

21. Bruce Sutherland, "Pittsburgh Volunteers with Sickles' Excelsior Brigade," *Western Pennsylvania Historical Magazine* 45 (Sept. 1962): 250–51.

22. John B. Gordon, *Reminiscences of the Civil War* (New York: Charles Scribner's Sons, 1903), 108–9.

23. Clement A. Evans, ed., *Confederate Military History, Extended Edition,* vol. 2, Maryland (Wilmington, N.C.: Broadfoot, 1987), 263–65; *History of the 118th Pennsylvania Volunteers* (Philadelphia: John L. Smith Map, 1905), 91–94.

24. See, for example, "A Neutral Cornfield and Its Reunions," *Forney's (Philadelphia) War Press,* Oct. 29, 1864, 7.

25. William McCarter, reminiscences, vol. 10, "My Life in the Army: 1862, Philadelphia, 1875," AM .6952, HSP, 39–40 (cited hereafter as McCarter reminiscences). McCarter served in Co. A of the 116th Pennsylvania Infantry.

26. Jesse Johnson, diary (Nov. 1861–July 1864), collection no. 1299, AM .6964, HSP. Johnson of New Salem, Fayette County, W. Va. was a private in Co. L, 2nd Regiment of West Virginia Cavalry (U.S.A.).

CHAPTER 2: FREEMASONRY AND ITS "BROTHERHOOD" IN THE CIVIL WAR

1. See James A. Congdon, Letters/Papers (1862–1865): Aug. 25, 1863; Sept. 17, 1863; Sept. 29, 1863; Oct. 3, 1863; Sept. 26, 1864, collection no. 1620, HSP.

2. Walter Symonds Newhall, letters (1862–1863), letter of Jul. 21, 1862, collection no. 1409, HSP.

3. Author's recollection; see also, Carroll Van West, *The Tennessee Encyclopedia of History and Culture* (Nashville: Tennessee Historical Society, 1998), 776.

4. See Frank Moore, "A Masonic Incident," in *The Civil War in Song and Story,* 1860–1865 (New York: P. F. Collier, 1889), 199–300; Julie Oliver, "A Brotherhood of Enemies," *Civil War Times Illustrated* 28, no. 7 (Jan./Feb. 1990): 74. "E. E. Cross" was Edward E. Cross, and James B. Perry was captain of Co. C.

5. Frederick C. Hitchcock, *War from the Inside: The Story of the 132nd Regiment of Pennsylvania Volunteers* (Philadelphia: J. B. Lippincott,

1904), 105–7; see also information on Lake, in Jeffry D. Wert, *Mosby's Rangers* (New York: Simon & Schuster, 1990), 184, 265–66.

6. Newton Martin Curtis, *From Bull Run to Chancellorsville: The Story of the Sixteenth New York Infantry Together with Personal Reminiscences* (New York: G. P. Putnam's Sons, 1906), 96–97.

7. Allen E. Roberts, *House Undivided: The Story of Freemasonry and the Civil War* (New York: Macoy Publishing & Masonic Supply, 1961), 118–19.

8. See, for example, the report of General Magruder for Feb. 26, 1863, of the event as contained in Clement A. Evans, ed., *Confederate Military History, Extended Edition,* vol. 15, Texas (1899; reprint, Wilmington, N.C.: Broadfoot, 1989.), 80–93; *Dictionary of American Biography,* vol. 19 (New York: Charles Scribner's Sons, 1937), 317–18 (cited hereafter as *DAB*); *The War of the Rebellion: A Compilation of the Official Records of the Union & Confederate Armies, Series 1,* vol. 15 (Washington, D.C.: Government Printing Office, 1886): 202–4 (cited hereafter as *OR*).

9. "An Affecting Incident," *Louisville (Ky.) Daily Journal,* Jan. 23, 1863, 4, col. 4.

10. "Incidents of the Battle of Galveston," *Louisville (Ky.) Daily Journal,* Feb. 16, 1863, 1, col. 1.

11. Roberts, *House Undivided,* 146.

12. Ibid., 147. For other accounts of Federal soldiers aiding Confederate soldiers and civilians on the basis of Freemasonry, see Roberts, *House Undivided,* 126, 152–54.

13. "Masonic Burial by an Enemy," *Confederate Veteran* 14, no. 9 (Sept. 1906): 408; Frederick Phisterer, *New York in the War of the Rebellion,* 3rd ed., vol. 4 (Albany, N.Y.: F. B. Lyon, 1912), 3, 3463; Edward W. Callahan, *List of Officers of the Navy of the United States and of the Marine Corps, from 1775 to 1900* (New York: L. R. Hammersly, 1901), 250. This book states that Lt. John E. Hart was "killed in battle," Jun. 11, 1863.

14. David Craft, *History of the One Hundred Forty-first Regiment, Pennsylvania Volunteers: 1862–1865* (Towanda, Pa.: Reporter-Journal, 1885), 81–83, 217.

15. "Grand Lodge of the Most Ancient and Honorable Fraternity of Free and Accepted Masons of Pennsylvania," Philadelphia, brochure presenting the Official Gettysburg Masonic Memorial Monument

Commemorative Collection; "Dedication Day in Gettysburg," *Pennsylvania Free Mason* 40, no. 3 (Aug. 1993): 1, 4.

16. Dr. Harry Caudill, interview with author, Lexington, Ky., Jan. 20, 1983.

17. St. Clair A. Mulholland, *Military Order: Congress Medal of Honor Legion of the United States* (Philadelphia: Town, 1905), 519–29.

18. Jeffry D. Wert, *Mosby's Rangers* (New York: Simon & Schuster, 1990), 244–47.

19. "Highly Creditable," *Danville (Va.) Sixth Corps,* 1, no. 15 (May 13, 1865): 2.

CHAPTER 3: REBELS AIDING YANKEES ON THE BATTLEFIELD

1. "Battle-Field Incident," *Philadelphia Grand Army Scout and Soldier's Mail* 3, no. 52 (Dec. 6, 1884): 3; C. A. Evans, *Confederate Military History,* vol. 2, Maryland, 296–97, 371–72.

2. F. Moore, *Civil War in Song,* 58.

3. J. W. Reid, *History of the Fourth Regiment of South Carolina Volunteers* (Greenville, S.C.: Shannon, 1892), 43–44.

4. *Confederate Veteran* 8, no. 2 (Feb. 1900): 67.

5. See Cumming, *A Journal of Hospital Life in the Confederate Army of Tennessee,* 14; William G. Stevenson, *Thirteen Months in the Rebel Army* (New York: A. S. Barnes & Burr, 1862), 156–58. Stevenson was in reality a Northerner who had been conscripted into the Rebel army.

6. "Death of a Union Soldier at Shiloh," *Confederate Veteran* 10, no. 4 (Apr. 1902): 163; William Kepler, *History . . . of the Fourth Regiment Ohio Volunteer Infantry* (Cleveland: Leader, 1886), 253. This history does not list a Sergeant Stevenson. A "John Burns," age eighteen, served in Co. C, and was discharged on a certificate of disability at Columbus, Ohio, Nov. 14, 1862 (Kepler, *History of the Fourth Regiment,* 253). The *Official Roster of the Soldiers of the State of Ohio in the War of the Rebellion,* 1861–1866, 12 vols. (Cincinnati: Wilstach and Baldwin, 1893–1895), 2: 97, records Burns's discharge on Mar. 14, 1862 for reasons of "disability."

7. Bruce Sutherland, "Pittsburgh Volunteers with Sickles' Excelsior Brigade," *Western Pennsylvania Historical Magazine* 45 (Sept. 1962): 65–66.

8. Joseph K. Newell, *Ours: Annals of 10th Regiment Massachusetts Volunteers, in the Rebellion* (Springfield, Mass.: C. A. Nichols, 1875), 35.

9. Gordon, *Reminiscences of the Civil War,* 108–9; Samuel P. Bates, *History of Pennsylvania Volunteers, 1861–5* 10 vols. (1869–71; reprint, Wilmington, N.C.: Broadfoot, 1993–94), 5:579, 581.

10. William H. Andrews, *Footprints of a Regiment: A Recollection of the 1st Georgia Regulars, 1861–1865* (Atlanta: Longstreet, 1992), 80–81; see also Andrews, *Footprints,* 204, n. 17.

11. "A Wounded Federal Color Bearer: From Report of His Experience—Sam Bloomer," *Confederate Veteran* 17 (Apr. 1909): 169.

12. John Quinn Imholte, *The First Volunteers: History of the First Minnesota Volunteer Regiment, 1861–1865* (Minneapolis: Ross & Haines, 1963), 141; *Minnesota in the Civil and Indian Wars, 1861–1865* (St. Paul: Pioneer Press, 1890), 1: 51; 2: 125–26.

13. "The Adventures of a Soldier," newspaper clipping (author, source, and date unknown) in scrapbook entitled "Newspaper Clippings Relating to the Civil War," call no. TL44448, HSP, 211.

14. *Philadelphia Public Ledger,* Oct. 30, 1862, 2, cols. 2–3; *Antietam to Appomattox with 118th Pennsylvania Volunteers:* Corn Exchange Regiment (Philadelphia: J. L. Smith, 1892), 737.

15. *Confederate Veteran* 2, no. 8 (Aug. 1894): 227.

16. *The Story of American Heroism: Thrilling Narratives of Personal Adventures During the Great Civil War* (Philadelphia: B. T. Calvert, 1897), 290–92; "He Gave His Enemy Drink," *Civil War Times Illustrated* 1, no. 6 (Oct. 1962): 38–39.

17. "Bravery of a Boy Soldier," *Confederate Veteran* 11, no. 2 (Feb. 1903): 57–58.

18. "He Gave His Enemy Drink," *Civil War Times Illustrated* 1, no. 6 (Oct. 1962): 39.

19. Mrs. Irvin H. McKesson, letter of Apr. 10, 1863, collection no. 1542, HSP.

20. W. R. Kiefer and Newton H. Mack, *History of the One Hundred and Fifty-third Regiment,* Pennsylvania (Easton, Pa.: Chemical, 1909), 178–79.

21. Craft, *History of the One Hundred Forty-first Regiment,* 129–130.

22. Levi W. Baker, *History of the Ninth Massachusetts Battery* (South Framingham, Mass.: Lakeview, 1888), 77–79.

23. A. L. Long and Marcus J. Wright, *Memoirs of Robert E. Lee: His Military and Personal History* (London: Sampson Low, Marston, Searle, & Rivington, 1886), 301–2.

24. *OR,* series 1, vol. 27, part 2, 468–69.

25. Ibid., 492–93.

26. See William Hanna, "The Barlow-Gordon Incident? The Yankee Never Met the Reb: A Gettysburg Myth Exploded," *Civil War Times Illustrated* 24, no. 3 (May 1985): 43–47. For a rebuttal to Hanna's thesis, see Glen W. Magnell, "Barlow-Gordon," *Civil War Times Illustrated* 24, no. 7 (Nov. 1985): 8; and "On the Battlefield: Meeting of Gen. Barlow and Senator Gordon at Gettysburg," *Lewistown (Pa.) Democratic Sentinel,* Mar. 6, 1879, 1, col. 6.

27. Gordon, *Reminiscences of the Civil War,* 151–53.

28. Many accounts exist of the "Gordon-Barlow" incident in various publications. See, for example: John Purifoy, "The Battle of Gettysburg, July 1, 1863," *Confederate Veteran* 31, no. 4 (Apr. 1923): 138–41; "The Brave Honor the Brave," *Confederate Veteran* 2, no. 5 (May 1894): 131–32; Champ Clark, *The Civil War: Gettysburg: The Confederate High Tide* (Alexandria, Va.: Time-Life Books, 1985): 60–61; "The Barlow-Gordon Incident," *Civil War Times Illustrated* 2, no. 4 (Jul. 1963): 48; *DAB* 1: 608.

29. "An Incident at Gettysburg: The Two Colonels," in *Histories of the Several Regiments and Battalions from North Carolina in the Great War, 1861–1865,* ed. Walter Clark (Goldsboro, N.C.: Nash Brothers, 1901), 611–16; Weymouth T. Jordan, Jr., and Louis H. Manarin, *North Carolina Troops: 1861–1865: A Roster,* vol. 10, Infantry (Raleigh, N.C.: Division of Archives and History, 1985), 293; *Official Army Register of the Volunteer Force of the United States Army for the Years 1861–1865,* part 7 (Washington, D.C.: Adjutant General's Office, 1867), 172.

30. L. W. Day, *Story of the One Hundred and First Ohio Infantry* (Cleveland: W. M. Bayne, 1894), 368.

31. William C. Brown, "How Confederates Treated a Federal," *Confederate Veteran* 13, no. 5 (May 1905): 228.

32. Theodore F. Allen, "The Underground Railroad and the Grapevine Telegraph: An Escaping Prisoner's Experience—1863," *MOLLUS* 6: 147–67.

33. Ibid., 150–52.

34. *Confederate Veteran* 7, no. 10 (Oct. 1899): 454.

35. Luther W. Hopkins, *From Bull Run to Appomattox: A Boy's View* (Baltimore: Fleet-McGinley, 1908), 147.

36. George S. Bernard, *War Talks of Confederate Veterans* (Petersburg, Va.: Fenn & Owen, 1892), 91–92.

37. Newell, *Ours,* 535–37.

38. G. W. Nichols, *A Soldier's Story of His Regiment: 61st Georgia* (Jesup, Ga., 1898), 186.

CHAPTER 4: YANKEES AIDING REBELS

1. A. S. Billingsley, *Christianity in the War* (Philadelphia: Claxton, Remsen, & Haffelfinger, 1872), 378.

2. "How Johnny Got Some Blankets," *Confederate Veteran* 16, no. 10 (Oct. 1908): 513.

3. *Philadelphia Public Ledger,* Sept. 18, 1881, 3, col. 7.

4. *A History of the Eleventh Regiment, Ohio Volunteer Infantry* (Dayton, Ohio: W. J. Shuey, 1866), 215–16.

5. *OR,* series 1, vol. 3, 291–92.

6. "Thrilling Story by a Union Veteran," *Confederate Veteran* 3, no. 12 (Dec. 1895): 383. This article erroneously uses "Newton" rather than "New Bern," as the place of battle. Mayo survived to become the major of the 4th North Carolina Cavalry (or 59th St. Troops), C.S.A. See Daniel H. Hill, *From Bethel to Sharpsburg,* vol. 1 (Raleigh, N.C.: Edwards & Broughton, 1926; reprint, Wilmington, N.C.: Broadfoot, 1992), 219–20.

7. James Grant, "The Flag and the Cross: A History of the United States Christian Commission," typescript, Feb. 1894, call no. AM .7905, HSP, 23. Records reveal that the dying Rebel soldier was actually John M. Jones, Co. C, 18th North Carolina Infantry, who was killed at Hanover Courthouse, Va., on May 27, 1862. See Jordan and Manarin, *North Carolina Troops,* vol. 6: Infantry, 338.

8. Charles A. Hale, "The Story of My Personal Experience at the Battle of Antietam," typescript, John R. Brooke Papers, 1870, collection no. 78, undated miscellaneous box, HSP; *Revised Roster of the Soldiers and Sailors of New Hampshire in the War of the Rebellion, 1861–1866* (Concord, N.H.: Ira C. Evans, Public Printer, 1895), 238.

9. Edward P. Smith, *Incidents of the United States Christian Commission* (Philadelphia: J. B. Lippincott, 1871), 43–44.

10. Bernard, *War Talks of Confederate Veterans,* xi, 25, 29–30.

11. Philip F. Brown, *Reminiscences of the War of 1861–1865* (Richmond: Whittet & Shepperson, 1917), 32–35.

12. *Story of American Heroism,* 247–49; Official Roster of the Soldiers of the State of Ohio in the War of the Rebellion: 1861–1866, 12 vols. (Akron: Werner, 1893–1895) 5: 520–24.

13. Jordan and Manarin, *North Carolina Troops,* vol. 7: Infantry, 187, 194.

14. Emil Rosenblatt and Ruth Rosenblatt, *Hard Marching Every Day: The Civil War Letters of Private Wilbur Fisk, 1861–1865* (Lawrence: University Press of Kansas, 1992), 362–63.

15. *Story of American Heroism,* 314–16.

16. *Confederate Veteran* 6, no. 2 (Feb. 1898): 73; Bates, *History of Pennsylvania Volunteers,* 7: 1198.

17. David Mouat, "Three Years in the Twenty-ninth Pennsylvania Volunteers, 1861–1864," file in 29th Regiment Pennsylvania Volunteers Papers, 1861–1900, collection no. 1808, HSP.

18. "A Wounded Confederate Prisoner," *Confederate Veteran* 6, no. 9 (Sept. 1898): 410; Lillian Henderson, *Roster of the Confederate Soldiers of Georgia, 1861–1865* Hapeville, Ga.: Longino & Porter, (1955–1958), 2: 235.

19. A. W. Bartlett, *History of the Twelfth Regiment New Hampshire Volunteers in the War of the Rebellion* (Concord, N.H.: Ira C. Evans, Printer, 1897), 423–24, and troop roster, 58.

20. Randolph W. Kirkland, Jr., *Broken Fortunes: South Carolina Soldiers . . . Who Died in the Service of their Country and State in the War for Southern Independence, 1861–1865* (Charleston, S.C.: South Carolina Historical Society, 1995), 42.

21. Charles H. Weygant, *History of the One Hundred and Twenty-Fourth Regiment. N.Y.S.V.* (Newburgh, N.Y.: 1877), 415–17; C. A. Evans, *Confederate Military History,* vol. 8, Alabama, 825.

22. Mulholland, *Military Order,* 427–30; Coles and Hartman, *Biographical Rosters of Florida's Soldiers,* 3: 875, 882.

23. *Confederate Veteran* 7, no. 10: 440.

24. "The Brave Honor the Brave," *Confederate Veteran* 2, no. 5 (May 1894): 131–32; *Confederate Veteran* 7, no. 4 (Apr. 1899): 179; Nelson W. Evans, *A History of Scioto County, Ohio* (Portsmouth, Ohio: Nelson W. Evans, 1903), 1073–74.

25. *Confederate Veteran* 7, no. 4: 165. George H. Blakeslee appears as a "Corporal" rather than captain, as stated in the article. He was discharged for disability on Feb. 1, 1863, prior to the battle of Peach Tree fought in 1864. There was a Capt. Samuel T. Walkley, Co. B,

129th Illinois Infantry, who captured a sword from a Confederate at this time. See *Report of the Adjutant General of the State of Illinois, 1861–1865* (Springfield: Baker, Bailhache, 1867), 2: 599; 7: 181; *OR,* series 1, vol. 38, part II: 22–25; 321–471.

26. "Battle Vignettes—In the Wilderness," *Crutch* 1, no. 25 (Jun. 25, 1864): 1.

27. "Colonel Cutcheon and the 20th Infantry," *Crutch* (Oct. 8, 1864).

28. Smith Papers, 262–63.

29. John R. Brink, "Three Long and Destructive Raids by Kautz's Cavalry," *Grand Army Scout and Soldier's Mail* 4, no. 8 (Jan. 31, 1885): 1; C. A. Evans, *Confederate Military History,* vol. 6: South Carolina, 635–36.

30. Thomas F. Dornblazer, *Sabre Strokes of the Pennsylvania Dragoons in the War of 1861–1865* (Philadelphia: Lutheran Publication Society, 1884), 193–97; C. A. Evans, *Confederate Military History,* vol. 7: Alabama, 272.

31. "Caring for a Wounded Enemy," *Confederate Veteran* 11, no. 4 (Apr. 1903): 163–64.

32. Mulholland, *Military Order,* 431–37.

33. Noble D. Preston, *History of the Tenth Regiment of Cavalry: New York State Volunteers* (New York: D. Appleton, 1892), 199–203.

34. Henderson, *Roster of Soldiers of Georgia,* 1:290.

35. Harry Gilmor, *Four Years in the Saddle* (New York: Harper & Brothers, 1866), 87–88.

36. "The Dead Man by the Roadside," *Crutch* (Jan. 14, 1864): 1.

CHAPTER 5: CIVILIANS AND SOLDIERS

1. James H. Walker, diaries (1861–1864), vol. 1 (Sept. 25, 1861–Sept. 1, 1862): 199–200, collection no. 1995, call no. AM .1122, HSP.

2. Elizabeth Avery Meriwether, *Recollections of Ninety-two Years, 1824–1916* (Nashville: Tennessee Historical Commission, 1958), 64–68.

3. Cornelia Barret Ligon, "Legend of the South," *American Heritage* 7, no. 4 (June 1956): 52–53, 108–11.

4. John Daniel Follmer, diary (1862–1865), typescript, call no. AM .66910, HSP.

5. Biddle letters. Mrs. Pollock's son was Capt. Thomas G. Pollock, who served on the staff of James L. Kemper's 7th Virginia. Captain Pollock was killed at Gettysburg on July 3, 1863.

6. Gordon, *Reminiscences of the Civil War,* 115–16.

7. "Confederate Necrology: Obituary: W. L. McLeod," *Georgia Historical Quarterly* 35 (Dec. 1951): 351.

8. "An Episode of the Late War," *Lebanon (Pa.) Courier,* Oct. 31, 1872, 1, col. 8; *Official Army Register,* part 8, Jul. 16, 1867, 186; Byron Sistler and Barbara Sistler, *1860 Census:Tennessee,* vol. 5 (Nashville: Byron Sistler and Associates, 1982), 302; *OR,* series 1, vol. 45, part 2, for miscellaneous data on Downey; "Davidson County, Tennessee, Slave Schedule Census, 1860" 5th Ward of Nashville, microfilm, series M-653, reel 1281, p. 252, National Archives Regional Library, Philadelphia. Downey actually enlisted as an officer in the 113th Ohio Infantry in Pickaway County, Ohio. See F. M. McAdams, *Everyday Soldier Life; or, a History of the One Hundred and Thirteenth Ohio Volunteer Infantry* (Columbus: Charles M. Cott, 1884), 172–73, 192, 246.

9. Clark letters.

10. Henry Y. Warnock, ed., *Sound of Drums: Selected Writings of Spencer B. King* (Macon, Ga.: Mercer University Press, 1984), 439.

11. "An Incident of the War," *Philadelphia Daily Age,* Aug. 28, 1865, 1, cols. 6–7; see *OR,* series 1, vol. 47, part 2, for scattered references to McQueen in South Carolina; Robert M. Kennedy and Thomas J. Kirkland, *Historic Camden: Nineteenth Century* (Columbia, S.C.: State, 1926), 2:170–75, 271, 374–76. The "poor old blind Bishop Davis" was the Reverend Thomas Frederick Davis of the Episcopal Theological Seminary in Camden, South Carolina.

12. Helen Styles, interview with author, Chester, Va., Apr. 24, 1996; Jordan and Manarin, *North Carolina Troops,* 4:285.

CHAPTER 6: PRISONS AND PRISONERS

1. James E. Rains, letter of Dec. 6, 1861, in Civil War: Confederate Generals, Simon Gratz Autograph Collection, case 5, box 16, HSP. The "Wildcat Fight" was an action at Rockcastle Hills or Camp Wild Cat, Ky., fought on Oct. 21, 1861.

2. John B. Lindsley, ed., *The Military Annals of Tennessee: Confederate* (Nashville: J. M. Lindsley, 1886), 290–96.

3. McCarter Reminiscences, Dec. 1875, vol. 8: 21–24.

4. *Philadelphia Public Ledger,* May 15, 1862, 1, col. 7; C. A. Evans, *Confederate Military History,* vol. 5: North Carolina, 508–10; James A. Emmerton, *A Record of the Twenty-third Regiment: Massachusetts*

Volunteer Infantry in the War of the Rebellion, 1861–1866 (Boston: William Ware, 1886), 107–8.

5. Frank T. Bennett, diary (1862), call no. AM .0819, HSP.

6. Julia Davis, *Never Say Die: The Glengarry McDonalds of Virginia* (Stafford, Va.: Northwood, 1980), 108.

7. "Reminiscences of a Federal Surgeon," *Confederate Veteran* 2, no. 12 (Dec. 1894): 356; 3, no. 2 (Feb. 1896): 52.

8. Herbert W. Beecher, *History of the First Light Battery: Connecticut Volunteers, 1861–1865: Personal Records and Reminiscences* (New York: A. T. De La Mare, 1901), 2:261, 791.

9. Louis N. Boudrye, *Historic Records of the Fifth New York Cavalry: First Ira Harris Guard* (Albany, N.Y.: S. R. Gray, 1865), 202, 252–54.

10. Thomas S. McCahan, diary (1862–1864), collection no. 1995, call no. AM .6092, HSP.

11. William Hyndman, *History of a Cavalry Company: A Complete Record of Company A, 4th Pennsylvania Cavalry* (Philadelphia: James B. Rodgers, 1870), 120–26.

12. "The Amenities of War," *Lewistown (Pa.) True Democrat,* Feb. 3, 1864, 1, col. 4. Incidentally, after the war, members of these organizations continued to hold reunions (see "A Very Happy Reunion," *New York Times,* Jul. 26, 1883, 5, col. 2); this article, however, states that the reunion was held by the 3rd rather than the 33rd Ohio.

13. Warnock, ed., *Sound of Drums,* 338–40; Henderson, *Roster of Soldiers of Georgia,* 1:857–58; Sarah Blackwell Gober Temple, *The First Hundred Years: A Short History of Cobb County in Georgia* (Atlanta: Walter W. Brown, 1935), 244, 574–75.

14. "Escaped Prisoner" *Louisville (Ky.) Daily Journal,* Mar. 20, 1865, 3, col. 2; *Tennessee in the Civil War: A Military History of Confederate and Union Units with Available Rosters of Personnel, in Two Parts,* part 2 (Nashville: Civil War Centennial Commission, 1965), 569.

15. Thomas J. Jordan, letters to wife Ella (1861–66), collection no. 2066, HSP.

16. "The Bravest Are the Gentlest," *Confederate Veteran* 31, no. 1 (Jan. 1923): 21.

17. Bates, *History of the Pennsylvania Volunteers,* 9:173; Samuel Clarke Farrar, *The Twenty-Second Pennsylvania Cavalry and the Ringold Battalion, 1861–1865* (Twenty-Second Pennsylvania Ringold Cavalry Association, 1911), 517.

18. Harry E. Smith, interview with author, Wilmington, Del., Oct. 14, 1995.

19. T. J. Mackey, "In Defense of the Enemy: Blue and Gray in the Same Line of Battle," from an undated, unnamed paper in a scrapbook entitled "Newspaper Clippings Relating to the Civil War," at HSP.

20. *OR,* series 1, vol. 41, part 1 of 4 parts, 434–39.

CHAPTER 7: FRIENDS AT THE BITTER END

1. Hunter Marshall, unpublished memoirs in author's possession. Robert H. Moore, II, *Chew's Ashby, ShoeMaker's Lynchburg, and the Newtown Artillery,* Virginia Regimental Histories Series, 111, 115.

2. Claiborne T. Smith, Jr., Dr., interview with author, Philadelphia, Mar. 19, 1993. See Claiborne T. Smith, *Smith of Scotland Neck: Planters on the Roanoke* (Baltimore: Gateway, 1976), 131.

3. Flint and Lee, "I Saw Lee Surrender," 27, 87–90.

4. Jeffry D. Wert, *General James Longstreet, The Confederacy's Most Controversial Soldier: A Biography* (New York: Touchstone Books, 1993), 402.

5. John Russell Young, "Grant Remembers Appomattox," in *Battle Chronicles of the Civil War: Leaders,* ed. James M. McPherson and Richard Gottlieb (New York: Macmillan, 1989), 77.

6. Warnock, ed., *Sound of Drums,* 388.

7. "The Final Salute at Appomattox," *Lewistown (Pa.) Gazette,* Jan. 4, 1894, 1, cols. 7–8.

8. Burke Davis, *Gray Fox: Robert E. Lee and the Civil War* (New York: Rinehart, 1956), 434–35.

9. *OR,* series 1, vol. 49, part 2.

10. See Warnock, ed., *Sound of Drums,* 344–46; "Trial of Henry Wirz," in *Executive Documents: The House of Representatives: 2nd Session, 40th Congress, 1867–68, no. 23* (Washington, D.C.: Government Printing Office, 1868), 384.

11. Henry Hurt, "Home of the Brave," *Reader's Digest* (May 1994): 69–73.

12. "Confederate Dead at Elmira Prison," *Confederate Veteran* 22 (1914): 396; Ausburn Towner, *Our Country and Its People: A History of the Valley and County of Chemung* (Syracuse, New York: D. Mason, 1892), 274–76.

CHAPTER 8: A BROTHERHOOD FOR THE ENEMY

1. *Philadelphia Public Ledger,* Jan. 4, 1850, 1, col. 7.

2. Ibid. Jan. 2, 1863, 2, col. 4.

3. Frank Wilkeson, *Recollections of a Private Soldier* (New York: Putnam, 1887), 232–35; Phillip Shaw Paludan, *Victims: A True Story of the Civil War* (Knoxville: University of Tennessee Press, 1981), 23.

4. Carlton McCarthy, *Detailed Minutiae of Soldier Life in the Army of Northern Virginia, 1861–1865* (Richmond, Va.: Carlton McCarthy, 1882), 102.

5. *Philadelphia Public Ledger,* Jan. 4, 1850, 1, col. 7.

6. "Triumphant 1868 March Proves Civil War is Over: Defeated Dixie Cheers Idealistic Sergeant and His Union Flag," *Philadelphia Inquirer,* Dec. 12, 1965, sec. 7, 6.

7. "Virginia Vets Enroute North," *Harrisburg (Pa.) Telegraph,* May 21, 1883; "Old Enemies Fraternizing," *Harrisburg (Pa.) Telegraph,* May 23, 1883.

8. "Pennsylvania Veterans in Virginia," *Harrisburg (Pa.) Telegraph,* May 23, 1883.

9. "A Call from the South: An Appeal from Robert E. Lee Camp, Confederate Veterans," *Wilmington (Del.) Every Evening,* Feb. 1, 1884, 1, col. 3.

10. Carol Reardon, *Pickett's Charge in History and Memory* (Chapel Hill: University of North Carolina Press, 1997): 191–92; "Two Gettysburg Encounters," *Literary Digest* 47 (Jul. 12, 1913): 75.

11. "A Touching Incident," *Elk County (Pa.) Advocate,* Oct. 1, 1874, 1, col. 4.

12. Ibid.

13. "A Confederate Funeral," *York (Pa.) Democratic Press,* June 27, 1862, 3, col. 1.

14. Edward L. Ayers, *The Promise of the New South: Life After Reconstruction* (New York: Oxford University Press, 1992), 332–33, 536, note 57.

15. Bruce Catton, *This Hallowed Ground: The Story of the Union Side of the Civil War* (New York: Pocket Books, 1956), 493.

16. *Henry V,* act 4, scene 3, lines 60–63, as published in G. R. Harrison, *Shakespeare: The Complete Works* (New York: Harcourt, Brace, Jovanovich, 1968), 761.

17. Robert Penn Warren, "A Mark Deep on a Nation's Soul," *Life Magazine* (Mar. 17, 1961): 88.

MONOGRAPHS

Andrews, William H. *Footprints of a Regiment: A Recollection of the 1st Georgia Regulars, 1861–1865.* Atlanta: Longstreet, 1992.

Ayers, Edward L. *The Promise of a New South: Life After Reconstruction.* New York: Oxford University Press, 1992.

Antietam to Appomattox with the 118th Pennsylvania Volunteers: Corn Exchange Regiment. Philadelphia: J. L. Smith, 1892.

Baker, Levi W. *History of the Ninth Massachusetts Battery.* South Framingham, Mass.: Lakeview, 1888.

Bartlett, A. W. *History of the Twelfth Regiment New Hampshire Volunteers in the War of the Rebellion.* Concord, N.H.: Ira C. Evans, 1897.

Bates, Samuel P. *History of the Pennsylvania Volunteers, 1861–1865.* 10 vols. 1869–71. Reprint, Wilmington, N.C.: Broadfoot, 1993–94.

Beecher, Herbert W. *History of the First Light Battery: Connecticut Volunteers, 1861–65: Personal Records and Reminiscences.* Vol. 2. New York: A. T. De LaMare, 1901.

Bernard, George S. *War Talks of Confederate Veterans.* Petersburg, Va.: Fenn & Owen, 1892.

Billingsley, A. S. *Christianity in the War.* Philadelphia: Claxton, Remsen & Haffelfinger, 1872.

Boudrye, Louis N. *Historic Records of the Fifth New York Cavalry: First Ira Harris Guard.* Albany, N.Y.: S. R. Gray, 1865.

Brochure Presenting the Official Gettysburg Masonic Memorial Monument Commemorative Collection. Philadelphia: Grand Lodge of the Most Ancient and Honorable Fraternity of Free and Accepted Masons of Pennsylvania, undated.

133

Brown, Philip F. *Reminiscences of the War of 1861–1865.* Richmond: Whittet & Shepperson, 1917.

Callahan, Edward W. *List of Officers of the Navy of the United States and of the Marine Corps, from 1775 to 1900.* New York: L. R. Hamersly, 1901.

Catton, Bruce. *This Hallowed Ground: The Story of the Union Side of the Civil War.* New York: Pocket Books, 1956.

Clark, Champ. *The Civil War: Gettysburg: The Confederate High Tide.* Alexandria, Va: Time-Life Books, 1985.

Clark, Walter, ed. *Histories of the Several Regiments and Battalions from North Carolina in the Great War, 1861–1865.* Goldsboro, N.C.: Nash Brothers, 1901.

Coles, David, and David Hartman. *Biographical Rosters of Florida's Confederate and Union Soldiers, 1861–1865.* 6 vols. Wilmington, N.C.: Broadfoot, 1995.

Craft, David. *History of the One Hundred Forty-first Regiment, Pennsylvania Volunteers, 1862–1865.* Towanda, Pa.: Reporter Journal, 1885.

Cumming, Kate. *A Journal of Hospital Life in the Confederate Army of Tennessee, from the Battle of Shiloh to the End of the War.* Louisville, Ky.: John P. Morton, 1866.

Curtis, Newton Martin. *From Bull Run to Chancellorsville: The Story of the Sixteenth New York Infantry Together With Personal Reminiscences.* New York: G. P. Putnam's Sons, 1906.

Davis, Burke. *Gray Fox: Robert E. Lee and the Civil War.* New York: Rinehart, 1956.

Davis, Julia. *Never Say Die: The Glengarry McDonalds of Virginia.* Stafford, Va.: Northwood, 1980.

Day, L. W. *Story of the One Hundred and First Ohio Infantry.* Cleveland: W. M. Bayne, 1894.

Delbruck, Hans. *History of the Art of War.* Translated by Walter J. Renfroe, Jr. Vol. 3. Westport, Conn.: Greenwood, 1982.

Dictionary of American Biography. 20 vols. New York: Charles Scribner's Sons, 1937.

Dornblazer, Thomas F. *Sabre Strokes of the Pennsylvania Dragoons in the War of 1861–1865.* Philadelphia: Lutheran Publication Society, 1884.

Dyer, Frederick H. *A Compendium of the War of the Rebellion.* Des Moines, Iowa: Dyer, 1908.

Emmerton, James A. *A Record of the Twenty-third Regiment: Massachusetts Volunteer Infantry in the War of the Rebellion, 1861–1865.* Boston: William Ware, 1886.

Evans, Clement A., ed. *Confederate Military History, Extended Edition.* 17 vols. 1899. Reprint, Wilmington, N.C.: Broadfoot, 1987–89.

Evans, Nelson W. *A History of Scioto County, Ohio.* Portsmouth, Ohio: Nelson W. Evans, 1903.

Farrar, Clarke. *The Twenty-Second Pennsylvania Cavalry and the Ringold Battalion, 1861–1865.* Twenty-Second Pennsylvania Ringold Cavalry Association, 1911.

Gilmor, Harry. *Four Years in the Saddle.* New York: Harper & Brothers, 1866.

Gordon, John B. *Reminiscences of the Civil War.* New York: Charles Scribner's Sons, 1903.

Henderson, Lillian. *Roster of the Confederate Soldiers of Georgia, 1861–1865.* 6 vols. Hapeville, Ga.: Longino & Porter, 1955–1958.

Hill, Daniel H. *From Bethel to Sharpsburg.* 2 vols. Raleigh, N.C.: Edwards & Broughton, 1926. Reprint, Wilmington, N.C.: Broadfoot, 1992.

History of the Eleventh Regiment, Ohio Volunteer Infantry, A. Dayton, Ohio: W. J. Shuey, 1866.

History of the 118th Pennsylvania Volunteers. Philadelphia: John L. Smith, Map, 1905.

Hitchcock, Frederick C. *War from the Inside: The Story of the 132nd Regiment Pennsylvania Volunteers.* Philadelphia: J. B. Lippincott, 1904.

Hopkins, Luther W. *From Bull Run to Appomattox: A Boy's View.* Baltimore: Fleet-McGinley, 1908.

Horn, Stanley F., ed. *Tennessee's War, 1861–1865: Described by Participants.* Nashville: Tennessee Civil War Centennial Commission, 1965.

Hyndman, William. *History of a Cavalry Company: A Complete Record of Company A, 4th Pennsylvania Cavalry.* Philadelphia: James B. Rodgers, 1870.

Imholte, John Quinn. *The First Volunteers: History of the First Minnesota Volunteer Regiment, 1861–1865.* Minneapolis: Ross & Haines, 1963.

Jordan, Weymouth T., Jr., and Louis H. Manarin. *North Carolina Troops, 1861–1865: A Roster.* 13 vols. Raleigh, N.C.: Division of Archives and History, 1985–1993.

Kennedy, Robert M., and Thomas J. Kirkland. *Historic Camden: Nineteenth Century.* 2 vols. Columbia, S.C.: State, 1926.

Kepler, William. *History . . . of the Fourth Regiment Ohio Volunteer Infantry.* Cleveland: Leader, 1886.

Kiefer, W. R., and Newton H. Mack. *History of the One Hundred and Fifty-third Regiment, Pennsylvania.* Easton, Pa.: Chemical, 1909.

Kirkland, Randolph W., Jr. *Broken Fortunes: South Carolina Soldiers . . . Who Died in the Service of Their Country and State in the War for Southern Independence, 1861–1865.* Charleston, S.C.: South Carolina Historical Society, 1995.

Lindsley, John B., ed. *The Military Annals of Tennessee: Confederate.* Nashville, Tenn.: J. M. Lindsley, 1886.

Long, A. L., and Marcus J. Wright. *Memoirs of Robert E. Lee: His Military and Personal History.* London: Sampson Low, Marston, Searle, & Rivington, 1886.

McAdams, F. M. *Everyday Soldier Life; or, A History of the One Hundred and Thirteenth Ohio Volunteer Infantry.* Columbus: Charles M. Cott, 1884.

McCarthy, Carlton. *Detailed Minutiae of Soldier Life in the Army of Northern Virginia, 1861–1865.* Richmond, Va.: Carlton McCarthy, 1882.

Meriwether, Elizabeth Avery. *Recollections of Ninety-two Years, 1824–1916.* Nashville: Tennessee Historical Commission, 1958.

Minnesota in the Civil and Indian Wars, 1861–1865. 2 vols. St. Paul: Pioneer Press, 1890.

Moore, Frank. *The Civil War in Song and Story, 1860–1865.* New York: P. F. Collier, 1889.

Moore, Robert H., II. *Chew's Ashby, Shoemaker's Lynchburg, and the Newtown Artillery.* Virginia Regimental Histories Series, undated.

Mulholland, St. Clair A. *Military Order: Congress Medal of Honor Legion of the United States.* Philadelphia: Town, 1905.

Newell, Joseph K. *Ours: Annals of 10th Regiment Massachusetts Volunteers, in the Rebellion.* Springfield, Mass.: C. A. Nichols, 1875.

Nichols, G. W. *A Soldier's Story of His Regiment: 61st Georgia.* Jesup, Ga., 1898.

Official Army Register of the Volunteer Force of the United States Army for the Years 1861–1865. Parts 7 and 8. Washington, D.C.: Adjutant General's Office, 1867.

Official Records of the War of the Rebellion . . . of the Union and Confederate Armies, Series 1. 53 vols. Washington, D.C.: Government Printing Office, 1880–1898.

Official Roster of the Soldiers of the State of Ohio in the War of the Rebellion, 1861–1866. 12 vols. 1893–1895.

Osborn, Donald Lewis. *Knowing the Bruners.* Lee's Summit, Mo., 1968.

Pauldan, Phillip Shaw. *Victims: A True Story of the Civil War.* Knoxville: University of Tennessee Press, 1981.

Phisterer, Frederick. *New York in the War of the Rebellion.* 3d ed. Vol. 4. Albany, N.Y.: F. B. Lyon, 1912.

Presidents, Soldiers, Statesmen. New York: H. H. Hardesty, 1889.

Preston, Noble D. *History of the Tenth Regiment of Cavalry: New York State Volunteers.* New York: D. Appleton, 1892.

Reardon, Carol. *Pickett's Charge in History and Memory.* Chapel Hill: University of North Carolina Press, 1997.

Reid, J. W. *History of the Fourth Regiment of South Carolina Volunteers.* Greenville, S.C.: Shannon, 1892.

Report of the Adjutant General of the State of Illinois, 1861–1865. Vols. 2 and 7. Springfield: Baker, Bailhache, 1867.

Revised Roster of the Soldiers and Sailors of New Hampshire in the War of the Rebellion, 1861–1866. Concord, N.H.: Ira C. Evans, Public Printer, 1895.

Roberts, Allen E. *House Reunited: Free Masonry Aids Reconstruction.* Highland Springs, Va.: Anchor Communications, 1996.

———. *House Undivided: The Story of Free Masonry and the Civil War.* New York: McCoy Publishing & Masonic Supply, 1961.

Rosenblatt, Emil, and Ruth Rosenblatt. *Hard Marching Every Day: The Civil War Letters of Private Wilbur Fisk, 1861–1865.* Lawrence: University Press of Kansas, 1992.

Shakespeare, William. *Henry V.,* in *Shakespeare: The Complete Works,* edited by G. R. Harrison. New York: Harcourt, Brace, Jovanovich, 1968.

Sistler, Byron, and Barbara Sistler. *1860 Census: Tennessee.* Vol. 5. Nashville: Byron Sistler & Associates, 1982.

Smith, Claiborne T. *Smith of Scotland Neck: Planters on the Roanoke.* Baltimore: Gateway, 1976.

Smith, Edward P. *Incidents of the United States Christian Commission.* Philadelphia: J. B. Lippincott, 1871.

Stevenson, William G. *Thirteen Months in the Rebel Army.* New York: A. S. Barnes & Burr, 1862.

Tennessee in the Civil War: A Military History of Confederate and Union Units with Available Rosters of Personnel, in Two Parts. Nashville: Civil War Centennial Commission, 1965.

Story of American Heroism: Thrilling Narratives of Personal Adventures during the Great Civil War, as Told by the Winners . . . , The. Philadelphia: B. T. Calvert, 1897.

Temple, Sarah Blackwell Gober. *The First Hundred Years: A Short History of Cobb County in Georgia.* Atlanta: Walter W. Brown, 1935.

Towner, Ausburn. *Our Country and Its People: A History of the Valley and County of Chemung.* Syracuse, N.Y.: D. Mason, 1892.

"Trial of Henry Wirz," in *Executive Documents: The House of Representatives: 2nd Session, 40th Congress, 1867–68. No. 23.* Washington, D.C.: Government Printing Office, 1868.

Tunnard, W. H. *A Southern Record: The History of the Third Regiment, Louisiana Infantry.* Baton Rouge, La.: 1866.

Uden, Grant. *A Dictionary of Chivalry.* Harmondsworth, England: Penguin Books, 1968.

Van West, Carroll. *The Tennessee Encyclopedia of History and Culture.* Nashville: Tennessee Historical Society, 1998.

Warnock, Henry Y., ed., *Sound of Drums: Selected Writings of Spencer B. King.* Macon, Ga.: Mercer University Press, 1984.

Wert, Jeffry D. *General James Longstreet: The Confederacy's Most Controversial Soldier: A Biography.* New York: Touchstone Books, 1993.

———. *Mosby's Rangers.* New York: Simon & Schuster, 1990.

Weygant, Charles H. *History of the One Hundred and Twenty-Fourth Regiment, N.Y.S.V.* Newburgh, N.Y.: 1877.

Wilkeson, Frank. *Recollections of a Private Soldier.* New York: Putnam, 1887.

Young, John Russell. "Grant Remembers Appomattox." In *Battle Chronicles of the Civil War: Leaders,* edited by James McPherson and Richard Gottlieb. New York: Macmillan, 1989.

MANUSCRIPTS

Note: "HSP" is the Historical Society of Pennsylvania in Philadelphia.

Bennett, Frank T., Col., 55th Pennsylvania Infantry. Diary (1862). Call no. AM .0189. HSP.

Biddle, James Cornell, 1st Lt., Company C and Company K, 27th Pennsylvania Infantry. Letters (1861–65) to his wife, Gertrude G. Meredith Biddle. Box 1. Collection no. 1881. HSP.

Boyts, Franklin, Company C, 142nd Pennsylvania Infantry. Diary (1862–65). Collection no. 1995, call no. AM .13752, in 4 volumes. HSP.

Clark, Thomas, Cpl., Company C, 97th Pennsylvania Infantry. Civil War Letters. Society Small Collection. HSP (cited hereafter as Clark letters).

Congdon, James A., Lt. Col., 113th Regiment, 12th Pennsylvania Cavalry. Letters/Papers (1862–65). Collection no. 1620. HSP.

"Davidson County, Tennessee, Slave Schedule Census, 1860" 5th Ward of Nashville. Microfilm, Series M-653, Reel 1281, p. 252. National Archives Regional Library, Philadelphia.

Follmer, John Daniel, Q.M., Company F, 161st Regt., 16th Pennsylvania Cavalry. Diary (1862–1865), typescript. Call no. AM .66910. HSP.

Grant, James. "The Flag and the Cross: A History of the United States Christian Commission" (Feb. 1894), typescript. Call no. AM .7905. HSP.

Green, John P., Asst. Adj. Gen. of Volunteers. "Personal Recollections of the Civil War" (Dec. 1914), unprocessed collection. HSP.

Hale, Charles A. "The Story of My Personal Experience at the Battle of Antietam," typescript. John Brooke Papers, 1870. Collection no. 78. Undated miscellaneous box. HSP.

Hopkinson, Oliver., Col., 1st Regiment, Delaware Infantry (also served in the 51st Pennsylvania Militia Regiment). Letters (1861–1863). "Autographs" in Hopkinson Papers. Collection no. 1978, vol. 19. HSP.

Johnson, Jesse. Company L, 2nd West Virginia Cavalry [U.S.A]. Diary (Nov. 1861–July 1864), typescript. Collection no. 1299, call no. AM .6964. HSP.

Jordan, Thomas J., Col., 9th Pennsylvania Cavalry. Letters to wife Ella (1861–66). Collection no. 2066. HSP.

Mackey, T. J., Capt. Engineers, C.S.A. "In Defense of the Enemy: Blue and Gray in the Same Line of Battle," from an undated, unnamed paper. Scrapbook entitled, "Newspaper Clippings Relating to the Civil War." Call no. TL 44448, 211. HSP.

Marshall, Hunter, Cpl. "The Beauregard Rifles: Shoemaker's Lynchburg [Virginia] Artillery," and "Stuart's Horse Artillery," [C.S.A.]. Unpublished memoirs in author's possession.

McCahan, Thomas S., Capt., Company M, 92nd Regiment, Ninth Pennsylvania Cavalry. Diary (1862–1864). Collection no. 1995, call no. AM .6092. HSP.

McCarter, William. Company A, 116th Pennsylvania Infantry. Reminiscences (Dec. 1875). Vols. 8 and 10. Collection no. 1307, call no. AM .6952. HSP.

McKesson, Mrs. Irvin H. Collection. no. 1542. HSP.

Newhall, Walter Symonds, Capt., Co. A, 60th Regiment, 3rd Pennsylvania Cavalry. Letters (1862–1863). Collection no. 1409. HSP.

Mitchell, John W. Letter in William Frederick Allen Civil War Correspondence (1860–1865), incoming, Company F., 38th Pennsylvania Infantry, 9th Reserve, transferred to 1st U.S. Cavalry. Collection no. 1919. HSP.

Moffit, John H. "Kriegsfangenen" (Prisoner of war). Manuscript in author's possession.

Mouat, David., Company G, 29th Pennsylvania Infantry. "Three Years in the Twenty-ninth Pennsylvania Volunteers, 1861–1864." File in 29th Regiment Pennsylvania Volunteers Papers (1861–1900). Collection no. 1808. HSP.

Rains, James E. Civil War Letter, Civil War: Confederate Generals, Simon Gratz Autograph Collection. Case 5. Box 16. HSP.

Smith, John L., Cpl., Company E, 91st Pennsylvania Infantry and Company K, 118th Pennsylvania Infantry Regiment (the Corn Exchange Regiment). Papers (book of mimeographed/carbon-copied Civil War letters [1862–65]; also miscellaneous loose original letters, diaries, letter books, etc.). Collection no. 610. HSP.

Sturgis, Abraham, Isaac Sturgis, James Sturgis, and William Sturgis. 1st Regt., Virginia Cavalry [U.S.A.] (the Pennsylvania Dragoons), 85th Pennsylvania Infantry, 14th Pennsylvania Cavalry. Letters (1861–64), typescript. Collection no. 831, call no. AM .2075. HSP.

Thompson, G. Earle, ed. "Diary of Sergeant Joseph M. Pattison: a Delaware Yank," (1864). *Society Miscellaneous Collection*. Typescript. HSP.

Walker, James H., Lt., Co. E, 81st Pennsylvania Infantry. Diaries (1861–1864). Collection no. 1995, call no. AM .1122. HSP.

NEWSPAPERS

Crutch

Danville (Va.) Sixth Corps

Elk County (Pa.) Advocate

Forney's (Philadelphia) War Press

Harrisburg (Pa.) Telegraph

Lebanon (Pa.) Courier

Lewistown (Pa.) Democratic Sentinel

Lewistown (Pa.) Gazette

Lewistown (Pa.) True Democrat

Louisville (Ky.) Daily Journal

New York Times

Philadelphia Daily Age

Philadelphia Grand Army Scout and Soldier's Mail

Philadelphia Inquirer

Philadelphia Public Ledger

Wilmington (Del.) Every Evening

York (Pa.) Democratic Press

ARTICLES

Allen, Theodore F. "The Underground Railroad and the Grapevine Telegraph: An Escaping Prisoner's Experience—1863." *MOLLUS* 6: 147–67.

"Barlow-Gordon Incident, The." *Civil War Times Illustrated* 2, no. 4 (July 1963): 48.

"Brave Honor the Brave, The." *Confederate Veteran* 2, no. 5 (May 1894): 131–32; 7, no. 4 (Apr. 1898): 179.

"Bravery of a Boy Soldier." *Confederate Veteran* 11, no. 2 (Feb. 1903): 57–58.

"Bravest Are the Gentlest, The." *Confederate Veteran* 31, no. 1 (Jan. 1923): 21.

"Confederate Dead at Elmira Prison." *Confederate Veteran* 22 (Sept. 1914): 396.

Brown, William C. "How Confederates Treated a Federal." *Confederate Veteran* 13, no. 5 (May 1905): 228.

"Caring for a Wounded Enemy." *Confederate Veteran* 11, no. 4 (Apr. 1903): 163–64.

"Confederate Necrology: Obituary: W. L. McLeod." *Georgia Historical Quarterly* 35 (Dec. 1951): 351.

Confederate Veteran 2, no. 8 (Aug. 1894): 227.

———— 6, no. 2 (Feb. 1898): 73.

———— 7, no. 4 (Apr. 1899): 165; no. 10 (Oct. 1899): 440, 454.

———— 8, no. 2 (Feb. 1900): 67.

"Death of a Union Soldier at Shiloh." *Confederate Veteran* 10, no. 4 (Apr. 1902): 163.

"Dedication Day in Gettysburg." *Pennsylvania Free Mason* 40, no. 3 (Aug. 1993): 1, 4.

DuVall, Gene. "A Most Memorable Christmas." *American Legion* (Dec. 1994): 24–25, 56.

Flint, Seth M., and William Rose Lee. "I Saw Lee Surrender." *Saturday Evening Post* 212, no. 41 (Apr. 6, 1940): 27, 87–90.

Hanna, William. "The Barlow-Gordon Incident? The Yankee Never Met the Reb: A Gettysburg Myth Exploded." *Civil War Times Illustrated* 24, no. 3 (May 1985): 43–47.

Hurt, Henry. "Home of the Brave." *Reader's Digest* (May 1994): 69–73.

"He Gave His Enemy Drink." *Civil War Times Illustrated* 1, no. 6 (Oct. 1962): 38–39.

"How Johnny Got Some Blankets." *Confederate Veteran* 16, no. 10 (Oct. 1908): 513.

Ligon, Cornelia Barret. "Legend of the South." *American Heritage* 7, no. 4 (June 1956): 52–53, 108–11.

Magnell, Glenn W. "Barlow-Gordon." *Civil War Times Illustrated* 24, no. 7 (Nov. 1985): 8.

"Masonic Burial by an Enemy." *Confederate Veteran* 14, no. 9 (Sept. 1906): 408.

Oliver, Julie. "A Brotherhood of Enemies." *Civil War Times Illustrated* 28, no. 7 (Jan./Feb. 1990): 74.

Purifoy, John. "The Battle of Gettysburg, July 1, 1863." *Confederate Veteran* 31, no. 4 (Apr. 1923): 138–41.

————. "The Brave Honor the Brave." *Confederate Veteran* 2, no. 5 (May 1894): 131–32.

"Reminiscences of a Federal Surgeon." *Confederate Veteran* 2, no. 12 (Dec. 1894): 356; 3, no. 2 (Feb. 1895): 52.

Sutherland, Bruce. "Pittsburgh Volunteers with Sickles' Excelsior Brigade." *Western Pennsylvania Historical Magazine* 45 (Sept. 1962): 65–66, 250–51.

"Thrilling Story by a Union Veteran." *Confederate Veteran* 3, no. 12 (Dec. 1895): 383.

"Two Gettysburg Encounters." *Literary Digest* 47 (July 12, 1913): 75.

Warren, Robert Penn. "A Mark Deep on a Nation's Soul." *Life Magazine* (Mar. 17, 1961): 88.

"Wounded Confederate Prisoner, A." *Confederate Veteran* 6, no. 9 (Sept. 1898): 410.

"Wounded Federal Color Bearer: From Report of His Experience—Sam Bloomer, A." *Confederate Veteran* 17, no. 4 (Apr. 1909): 169.

MISCELLANEOUS SOURCES

Caudill, Dr. Harry. Interview with author, Lexington, Ky., Jan. 20, 1983.

Rolph, Barbour R. Correspondence with author, July 24, 1980.

Smith, Claiborne T., Jr., Dr. Interview with author, Philadelphia, Mar. 19, 1993.

Smith, Harry E. Interview with author, Wilmington, Del., Oct. 14, 1995.

Styles, Helen. Interview with author, Chester, Va., Apr. 24, 1996.

INDEX

Page numbers in italics indicates illustrations.